103 FUN WAYS TO ENJOY RETIREMENT LIKE A KING

A Unique Gift for Men Who Retired from Work, Not from Fun

REBEL BOOMERS INK

TABLE OF CONTENTS

Introduction 5

Alarm Clocks Are Cancelled — Welcome to the Life You Were Meant to Live

Chapter 1: No More Bosses—Just Chill Days 9

Because early alarms and office politics are officially canceled.

Chapter 2: Vibrancy and Rebellion: How to Retire Like a Rockstar 27

You didn't come this far to go quiet.

Chapter 3: Extreme Travel Adventures for the Retired King 47

Extreme travel stories your grandkids won't believe.

Chapter 4: Friends, Fun, and Fresh Starts—Social Adventures That Spark Joy and Connection 67

Connection, chaos, and backyard legends.

Chapter 5: Out of the Comfort Zone, Into the Legend—Bold Adventures That Change You 87

Growth looks better with a little danger.

Chapter 6: Master Something New—Creative and Modern Skills to Reignite Passion and Purpose 107

Learn something new. Then make it badass.

Chapter 7: The King's Giveback—Powerful Ways to Volunteer, Serve, and Build Community ....

Build a legacy that's bigger than your backyard.

Chapter 8: Wander Boldly—Wild and Spontaneous Adventures for the Open-Road Soul 143

For the open-road soul and the one-way-ticket spirit.

Conclusion: Long Live the King of Retirement 165References 168

© Copyright 2025 - All rights reserved.

The content contained within this book may not be reproduced, duplicated or transmitted without direct written permission from the author or the publisher.

Under no circumstances will any blame or legal responsibility be held against the publisher, or author, for any damages, reparation, or monetary loss due to the information contained within this book, either directly or indirectly.

Legal Notice:

This book is copyright protected. It is only for personal use. You cannot amend, distribute, sell, use, quote or paraphrase any part, or the content within this book, without the consent of the author or publisher.

Disclaimer Notice:

Please note the information contained within this document is for educational and entertainment purposes only. All effort has been executed to present accurate, up to date, reliable, complete information. No warranties of any kind are declared or implied. Readers acknowledge that the author is not engaged in the rendering of legal, financial, medical or professional advice. The content within this book has been derived from various sources. Please consult a licensed professional before attempting any techniques outlined in this book.

By reading this document, the reader agrees that under no circumstances is the author responsible for any losses, direct or indirect, that are incurred as a result of the use of the information contained within this document, including, but not limited to, errors, omissions, or inaccuracies.

INTRODUCTION

Alarm Clocks Are Cancelled—Welcome to the Life You Were Meant to Live

Hey there, future retiree! Yes, you. The guy who's finally stepping off the hamster wheel of nine-to-five, ready to trade in spreadsheets for spectacular sunsets and conference calls for cocktails on the coast. You've spent years being anything but ordinary, and retirement shouldn't change that. In fact, it's your grand opportunity to redefine what this phase of life means—not just for yourself, but for every other man who won't settle for a rocking chair.

I want you to picture yourself waking up when your body decides it's time, not when an alarm insists. Your schedule? Nonexistent. Your plans? Whatever you fancy. Retirement is your golden ticket, a passport to 103 incredible and unconventional adventures that await your fearless spirit and bold heart. Perhaps you're wondering if such a retirement is possible or even realistic. Well, I'm here to tell you that it absolutely is. Just think about it: After decades tethered to obligations, what does a day of freedom look like?

Maybe it's ditching the mundane for a cross-country road trip in a vintage car, or finally picking up that guitar to woo an audience beyond the shower walls. This book invites you to see retirement as the exhilarating next chapter, filled with laughter and camaraderie, rather than the closing of a book.

Retirement isn't just stepping away from the workforce; it's stepping into a new world of freedom where spontaneity reigns supreme. And yes, while escaping the work grind can be thrilling, it can also bring a wave of emotions you didn't quite expect. Some days might feel like a roller coaster ride, but remember, every good story has its twists, and this one belongs to you.

Who says retirement has to mean slowing down? It's about speeding up toward experiences you've postponed for too long. How about painting vibrant landscapes that rival Monet? Or brewing the perfect cup of coffee in some quaint foreign town? Maybe it's sailing across pristine waters with the wind at your back and nothing but adventure ahead. Each experience unfolds as naturally as turning a page in a gripping novel, and oh, what a story your retirement will be.

This isn't just another guide, it's your road map to carving out a legendary life chapter filled with creativity, exploration, rebellion, and, most importantly, fun. Together, we'll move through 103 wildly enjoyable ways to change your days into exciting adventures. Each chapter will spotlight a theme to spark inspiration and activities that shatter convention and awaken the daring part of you that's been waiting for its moment.

So, why hide under the label of "quiet grandpa" when you're destined for more? Embrace mischief, seek thrills, and enjoy those unexpected jaunts to places you've never been, both literally and figuratively. Whether it's learning how to surf, taking improv classes, joining a band, or even starting a quirky business venture, each idea is designed to reignite your zest for life.

Remember, the best stories are lived, not told. Retire like a king, not on a throne, but on a crest of waves, in a room full of laughter, or atop mountains you've yet to climb. Every adventure is a testament to living boldly, and this book is your gateway to doing just that.

And so, the time has come to grab your sense of humor, a willingness to break the mold, and step into this next chapter brimming with possibilities.

It's going to be epic!

CHAPTER 1

NO MORE BOSSES—
JUST CHILL DAYS

Welcome to the golden hour of your life, where "I have a meeting" now means meeting your hammock at 2 p.m. sharp, and the only deadlines that matter are the early bird dinner specials. This chapter is all about savoring your glorious escape from the nine-to-five jungle and leaning into the sweet, smooth jazz of chill days, spontaneous fun, and unapologetic freedom.

You've officially clocked out for the last time. No more expense reports, traffic jams, or passive-aggressive reply-all emails from Debra in accounting. You're the captain now, of your own schedule, your own joy, and your own damn destiny. So, what do you do with all this open space? Anything, everything, or absolutely nothing.

This chapter is all about waking up excited again, not to hustle, but to wander. Whether you're planning a legendary retirement send-off (think party + passport), learning to nap like an Italian, or finding the bliss in a long walk with no destination, we're going to explore how to make your days feel like a deep breath after decades of holding it all in.

So, kick off those uncomfortable work shoes, put your feet up, and let's celebrate the unscheduled, unapologetically chill life you've entered. No more bosses. No more rules. Just days that are fully, joyfully yours.

I

Throw Yourself a Modern Retirement Party (Yes, With a Hashtag)

Ditch the plain sheet cake in the break room; it's time for a truly memorable farewell as you transition into a newfound era of freedom. Consider renting a spacious rooftop bar to soak in stunning views or booking a food truck that serves your favorite cuisine to delight your guests. If you're feeling adventurous, hire a local DJ to get the party vibe going—though if you prefer, you could even take on the role yourself. Don't forget to send out vibrant digital invitations through platforms like Evite or Paperless Post, crafting something striking and unconventional. Create a distinct party hashtag such as #EpicRetirementJourney or #FreeAtLast, encouraging friends and family to document the festivities through photos. For added excitement, set up a "Past Life Burn Box" and invite guests to jot down old stressors or work-related annoyances on paper and safely burn them in a fire pit, all while toasting with s'mores. This celebration marks not the end of a career, but the exhilarating beginning of your next chapter. Revel in the reality of a life free from early morning emails. You're the man of the hour, you deserve multiple toasts, perhaps even a crown—because why not?

Go on a "Yes Day" Adventure

You know that scene in every road trip movie where the guy finally lets loose, says yes to everything, and ends up zip-lining in Costa Rica with a stranger named Larry? It's your turn. Pick a day, any day, and call it your personal "Yes Day." Say yes to that spontaneous invite to a food truck fest. Yes to the funky hat at the thrift store. Yes to karaoke, even if you only know the chorus. Your only job is to explore, laugh, and do something completely out of the ordinary. You're not on a schedule anymore. You're not living for weekends. You *are* the weekend now. Use websites like Eventbrite or Meetup to find quirky events near you—from goat yoga to indie film festivals. Make it a solo day or bring your ride-or-die crew. Either way, pack snacks and curiosity. Freedom tastes best with a little spontaneity sprinkled on top.

3

Learn to Ride a Motorcycle (Or a Fancy Electric Scooter)

Now that you've traded in your beige sedan and the stress of commuting while listening to traffic reports, consider switching from four wheels to two. Taking motorcycle lessons is not merely a midlife cliché; it's an exhilarating passport to the joy of feeling the wind in your hair. You might want to explore options like Harley-Davidson's Riding Academy or find a local motorcycle safety course to get started. For those who lean toward a more modern form of rebellion, there are stylish electric scooters available, such as the sleek NIU scooters or the iconic Vespa electrics. Either choice you make will ensure that you embody the essence of cool, reminiscent of a *Retirement Weekly: The Cool Edition* cover star. A helpful tip: While leather jackets are not a requirement, sunglasses are a must-have accessory. The freedom is yours to embrace now. Ride to the grocery store for no reason, chase after the sunrise, or simply hit the road to feel truly alive. It's all about savoring that sense of freedom and maybe even looking like a badass in the process.

4

Take a One-Way Ticket (Just for the Thrill)

Now that no boss is watching your vacation days stack up like dusty library books, it's time to book that one-way ticket. Not because you're running away, but because you can. Buy a one-way flight to a city you've never been to. Start with a place that's got flavor like New Orleans, Lisbon, Tokyo. Don't overplan. Just go, explore, and eat what the locals eat. Dance where they dance. Stay until your socks are worn out. Apps like Skyscanner and Hopper can help you snag deals, and Airbnb Experiences can add some local flavor. The goal? Reclaim your sense of wild curiosity. Your 30s were for climbing ladders. Your 40s were for raising humans. This chapter? It's for walking unfamiliar streets, ordering espresso in bad Spanish, and finding out you like it black with sugar. Take a journal. Call it your King's Log. Write stories that your younger self would high-five you for.

Create a No-Alarm Clock Rule (Then Watch What Happens)

After decades of waking up to the incessant buzz of alarm clocks disrupting your dreams, it's time to take a stand. Embrace the freedom of a new house rule: no alarm clocks—unless you choose to use one. Let your body rhythm align with the rise and fall of the sun, your hunger cues, or even that whimsical urge to whip up some pancakes in the morning. It's a delightful act of rebellion wrapped in flannel pajamas. To make an even bolder statement, consider donating your old alarm clock to Goodwill, and include a cheeky note that reads, "It's not me, it's you." Utilize apps like Sleep Cycle to track your sleep patterns, discovering how your natural rhythms shift when you are free from the constraints of an alarm. You may find that your dreams become more vivid, your thoughts clearer, and you wake up bursting with creativity, filled with ideas for poetry or delicious omelets. Retirement is not merely about reducing your activity, but rather about reclaiming your time to welcome life at your own pace. Notice the change in your energy levels when your morning begins with a gentle stretch rather than hitting the snooze button.

6

Try Solo Dining at a Five-Star Restaurant

Dining alone is a prospect that intimidates many, but not you. As a retired man with a bold spirit, you welcome the opportunity to transform into the enigmatic figure savoring a glass of red wine at the chef's table. This is your time to shine. Take a moment to call a local fine-dining establishment or browse through OpenTable to secure a reservation. Make sure to dress sharply; your attire sets the tone for the evening. Bring along a book or notepad to immerse yourself in your thoughts or jot down reflections. There's no need for the façade of pretending to send texts; this meal is about you, your experiences, and the delectable duck confit that awaits. To elevate the occasion further, ask your waiter for suggestions on what they would order if money were no object. Allow them to guide your culinary journey. With this newfound freedom, there's no need to rush through your meal or share your appetizer. Instead, you can take your time, indulging in every bite as if you're a king in his castle, relishing each moment of your well-deserved dinner.

7

SIGN UP FOR SOMETHING YOU NEVER GOT TO DO AS A KID

Remember that dream you always had but put on the back burner while moving through the demands of adulthood? Perhaps it was taking guitar lessons, trying your hand at fencing, joining the astronomy club, or mastering archery. Now is the perfect moment to pursue those interests you once set aside. Look to CourseHorse, your local community center, or even explore YouTube University to find the perfect starting point. Rekindling your passion for learning just because it fills you with excitement is a joy that many have neglected, but it's experiencing a revival among retirees. If you're ready to aim high, consider blacksmithing or glassblowing at The Crucible in Oakland; you might be astonished at how quickly that feeling of indifference fades when you find yourself wielding a sword you crafted yourself or strumming the opening chords of "Sweet Home Alabama." Embracing this newfound freedom means reigniting those childhood passions and turning them into the fires of adulthood.

8

REDESIGN YOUR LIVING SPACE FOR FUN, NOT FUNCTION

You no longer need a "home office." Dismantle that traditional desk setup and change the space into a haven of your own choosing. Picture a poker den where friends gather, a cozy lounge for immersive record listening, or even an indoor putting green to hone your skills. Welcome the unconventional; this is your retirement lair. Seek inspiration from IKEA hacks on YouTube or minimalist transformations featured on Apartment Therapy. Consider adding a hammock for relaxation or displaying art that evokes joy or intrigue. Daringly paint one wall a hue that challenges your comfort zone, something that excites you just a bit. The aim is to create an environment that reflects your personality—playful, engaging, and carefree. Every inch of your abode should resonate with the message, "I can finally enjoy this space without the hassle of printer cartridges." This is the time to mold your surroundings into the perfect backdrop for the next chapter of your life, one that truly inspires you.

9

START A FREEDOM JAR

Your *Reverse Swear* Jar

Take a jar and label it "Freedom Fund." Each time you make a spontaneous decision—whether it's skipping a shave, indulging in a midday nap, or declining an invitation to a mundane event, throw a few dollars into that jar. At the end of the month, treat yourself by utilizing that cash for a well-deserved mini splurge. Maybe hit up a round of golf, buy a concert ticket, or book a last-minute massage. This practice goes beyond mere monetary savings. It serves as a daily reminder that you truly own your time now. To take it a step further, consider using an app like Qapital, which automates your savings every time you bypass something unessential. Change these brief moments of freedom into significant, enjoyable rewards. Remember, retirement isn't solely about saving every last penny; it's about accumulating experiences that make you beam with joy, much like a teenager who just got their driver's license for the first time.

10

Say Yes to the Matinee and the Popcorn Upgrade

You no longer need to wait for weekends or endure the hassle of crowded theaters. The allure of weekday matinees is irresistible, offering movies at half the price and with double the legroom. Gather your fellow movie enthusiasts or enjoy some quality time on your own. Yes, there will be popcorn, and of course, you'll be sinking into a recliner seat for optimal comfort. Many theaters, such as Alamo Drafthouse and Cinemark, provide great early-day deals, senior discounts, and even offer beer and food service to enhance your cinematic experience. Consider making this a regular event—Matinee Monday or Film Buff Friday. These simple pleasures, once reserved for special occasions, will become treasured rituals. Keep in mind that just because your workday has ended doesn't mean the fun has to stop. On the contrary, this period can transform into your personal movie montage. Enjoy every moment, grease-stained hands and all. It's time to celebrate the joy of cinema!

MASTER THE ART OF JUST BROWSING AT A MUSEUM, NOT A MALL

Visit a museum on a slow Tuesday morning. There are no kids to distract you, no crowds to overwhelm you—just you and a world of ancient artifacts, modern art, or even dinosaur bones. The universe is filled with beautiful oddities, and now you finally have the chance to take it all in without any pressure to hurry. Discover hidden treasures through Atlas Obscura, or check if your city hosts "suggested donation" days for major museums where you can explore without breaking the bank. Stroll through the exhibits at a leisurely pace. Take the time to read each plaque and absorb the stories behind the artifacts. Find a bench where you can sit and observe fellow visitors, as if it's your new favorite pastime. You might stumble upon a newfound passion for glass art, or you might simply savor the delicious croissants at the café. Regardless of what you uncover, you'll walk away feeling richer in experience than when you walked in. Culture reigns supreme, and now you wear the crown, and you have the time to enjoy it all.

12

BECOME A LOCAL LEGEND AT YOUR FAVORITE COFFEE SPOT

Select a local café that embodies authenticity, a place that churns out genuine vibes, not a faceless chain. Look for that establishment with vinyl records spinning softly in the background and a chalkboard menu that changes with the seasons. Make it a habit to frequent this spot regularly. Order your favorite drink until the staff knows not just your name, but the stories that define you. Engage in conversations with the baristas; exchange jokes and anecdotes, and bring a journal to jot down your thoughts. It's time to change into *that* guy—the relaxed, insightful figure admired for his humor and enigmatic interests. This time in your life goes beyond just consuming caffeine; it's about constructing your personal realm, one interaction and flaky croissant at a time. Many local cafés host lively open-mic nights, book clubs, or trivia events. Don't hesitate to ask about them and participate actively. Use resources like Yelp or LocalCoffeeShops.com to discover your new favorite hangout. In a fast-paced world, choose to pause, enjoy your drink, and forge meaningful connections.

Carl's Retirement Party Broke the Internet and Maybe His Neighbor's Lawn Flamingo

Carl Donnelly, 67, spent 38 years working in municipal IT, keeping the town's ancient computers alive with little more than duct tape, dry wit, and vending machine snacks. His retirement was looming, and while his coworkers offered to get him the standard sheet cake and sad balloon combo in the break room, Carl had other plans.

"Oh, I'm not going out with a whimper," he declared. "I'm going out with a DJ, a taco truck, and a hashtag."

His daughter, a marketing manager with a flair for chaos, helped him plan what would soon be known as #CarlsFree—a retirement bash so extra, it had its own Instagram story highlight reel.

He rented out a rooftop brewery with sweeping views of the city. Invitations went out via Paperless Post, featuring an animated GIF of Carl doing finger guns in front of a stock photo of a beach. The dress code? "Business casual from the waist up, party animal from the waist down."

Carl wore a velvet smoking jacket, cargo shorts, and aviators. He topped it off with a bedazzled Burger King crown that said "King of Quitting."

The DJ (a college kid named DJ Phresh Lettuce) opened with ABBA and ended with Lizzo. Carl took the mic halfway through the night, made a toast with a margarita in each hand, and shouted, "No more conference calls, Susan!" to thunderous applause. Susan, his longtime work frenemy, graciously raised her glass.

But the real star? The "Past Life Burn Box." Guests scribbled down their biggest work annoyances on neon sticky notes:

- "Micromanaging Mondays"
- "Ted from Accounting's chewing"
- "Reply-all disasters"

Carl himself wrote: "That printer I fought for 11 years. You know what you did."

Then, they tossed the notes into a fire pit while making s'mores and dancing to Earth, Wind & Fire.

By 10 p.m., someone posted a slow-mo video of Carl doing the worm on TikTok. It hit 40K views by sunrise.

The next morning, slightly hungover and still wearing one of the taco truck's sombreros, Carl sat in a deck chair with no inbox, no responsibilities, and one very epic memory.

His first official act as a retiree? Changing his Wi-Fi name to "NoMore9to5."

Because retirement isn't the end—it's the afterparty of your entire career. And yes, you absolutely deserve a hashtag.

Final Thoughts: Leaving Work Behind

You've left your work life behind. The goal of this chapter was to offer you suggestions to gently switch gears. From rigid schedules to freedom and relaxation. From blaring alarm clocks to coffee shop chatter.

Let me ask you this: Are you ready to turn it up a notch? Let's move into the next chapter and dive into the excitement this new phase in your life can bring!

CHAPTER 2

VIBRANCY AND REBELLION: HOW TO RETIRE LIKE A ROCKSTAR

ENJOY RETIREMENT LIKE A KING

Let's be honest—when you pictured retirement, you weren't fantasizing about beige cardigans, lukewarm bingo nights, or "early bird specials" at 4 p.m. Nah. You've done the polite thing. You played the responsible role. You showed up, worked hard, raised people, paid taxes, and maybe even coached a Little League team or assembled IKEA furniture without losing your mind.

Now? Now it's your encore.

This chapter is all about shaking things up and retiring like the legend you are. We're talking about flipping the script, challenging the idea that aging means slowing down, and trading "golden years" for something more like platinum. This is about vibrancy, rebellion, and unapologetic joy. This is about throwing a metaphorical guitar through the window of retirement stereotypes and saying, "I'll take mine loud, thank you very much."

Let's burn the retirement rulebook and turn up the volume, shall we?

13

Get a Tattoo (Even a Tiny One)

You've navigated through faxes, flip phones, and various fashion trends, and now the time has come to etch your legacy in ink. A tattoo doesn't have to be an elaborate full sleeve unless that's what you're passionate about—but hey, props to you if it is. A simple minimalist piece, like a compass, a roaring lion, or even the initials of your grandchild on your wrist, boldly declares, *I'm still crafting my narrative.* To start, find a reputable tattoo shop on platforms like TattooDo or browse through an artist's portfolio on Instagram for inspiration. Keep in mind that some shops offer numbing cream to ease any concerns about pain. Ultimately, this ink isn't an act of defiance against the world, it's a personal statement of rebellion for yourself. It stands for all those years you played it safe and symbolizes a newfound freedom to be bold. So go ahead, get inked, flash that grin, and gather stories that are uniquely yours.

14

Rock the Style You Never Had the Nerve to Try

Have you ever had a hidden desire to rock leather pants with an air of confidence? Or perhaps those vibrant sneakers that catch the eye? Maybe even a fedora that exudes charisma without shouting, "I'm wealthy"? This is your chance to redefine your wardrobe and showcase your true self. Step into a boutique and consult with a stylist. Yes, there are experts for men. Consider checking out Bonobos or Stitch Fix Men, or arrange for a session with a local fashion consultant who can elevate your style game. It's time to add a bold jacket that speaks volumes, snag that unique ring that represents your personality, and experiment with patterns that make a statement. Envision yourself as the stylish villain in a gripping spy film who commands attention and intrigue. No longer are you dressing merely for work meetings; instead, you're curating a look meant for adventures, unforgettable moments, and an irresistible magnetic energy that draws people in.

Take the Stage—Open Mic Style

You possess a wealth of wisdom, a sharp wit, and narratives that surpass the offerings of many 20-something comedians currently performing stand-up. So, why not share this gift with others? Seek out an open mic night at a local bar or café. Resources like OpenMicFinder can help you locate an event near you. Once you've found a venue, go ahead and sign up to present your comedy, storytelling, or even spoken word piece. If the thought of stepping onto that stage feels intimidating, consider taking a stand-up workshop beforehand. Esteemed institutions like The Second City provide beginner courses tailored for newcomers. Remember, your aim isn't to simply "kill" the audience with laughter; rather, you're there to embrace the thrill of being alive and sharing your voice. And hey, if you happen to make someone in the crowd laugh so hard that their drink comes shooting out of their nose, you've instantly earned some bonus points for your performance!

16

Build a Custom Motorcycle or Classic Car

Do you have grease coursing through your veins? It's time to embrace the exhilarating world of fast and free. Consider purchasing a fixer-upper and transforming it into your ultimate dream machine. Local auto clubs or websites such as Bring a Trailer and Revival Cycles serve as hidden treasures for finding classic car or motorcycle restoration projects just waiting for a new life. Don't have a garage to work in? No worries—team up with a community workshop or a fellow gearhead who shares your passion. Remember, this journey extends beyond just the engine; it's about meticulously crafting a beast that proudly proclaims, *This ride is mine.* Even if your creation never reaches top speed on the open road, the true freedom lies in the process. You'll experience the thrill of your hard work paying off and the undeniable envy from others who see your masterpiece. So, roll up your sleeves and get ready to dive into a project that reflects your style and spirit.

17

LAUNCH A BOLD SIDE HUSTLE

Retired? Pfft. That doesn't mean you're expired. Instead, it's a golden opportunity to transform your hobby into a swagger-filled side hustle that keeps your spirit alive and thriving. Why not sell those unique, hand-carved cigar ashtrays that you've been crafting? Or consider making custom guitar straps that resonate with your personal flair? Perhaps you could even offer "badass grandpa" BBQ classes, sharing your grilling secrets with those eager to learn. Welcome this chance to defy the conventional notion that retirement equates to stagnation and unproductivity. You now have the liberty to work on *your* terms, managing your passion projects while enjoying life to the fullest. Utilize platforms like Etsy, Fiverr, or Facebook Marketplace to showcase your creations and skills. Not only can you engage in activities that you truly love, but you also might find yourself making some extra cash, whether it be beer money, whiskey money, or enough for that hot tub upgrade you've been eyeing. You get the idea; it's time to turn your downtime into something extraordinary!

18

Go Axe Throwing With Your Crew

This activity embodies a primal essence that blends absurdity with electrifying fun. Gather your crew and secure a group session at an axe-throwing venue such as Bad Axe Throwing or Urban Axes. Once inside, immerse yourselves in an atmosphere filled with camaraderie, laughter, and healthy competition. Feel the adrenaline pumping through your veins as you hurl axes at the targets, channeling the spirit of a Viking warlord. Each throw ignites a sense of exhilaration, making you feel invincible, like a warrior who has just returned from a victorious battle. Don't forget to wear your favorite flannel shirt to complete the look and perhaps even channel Thor's thunderous charisma as you banter with your friends. The experience isn't merely about throwing axes; it's about embracing the raw power within, surrounded by the sounds of laughter and the scent of victory in the air. Retirement isn't a soft landing; it's a fierce journey filled with steel, wood, and an adrenaline surge that brings out the warrior in all of us.

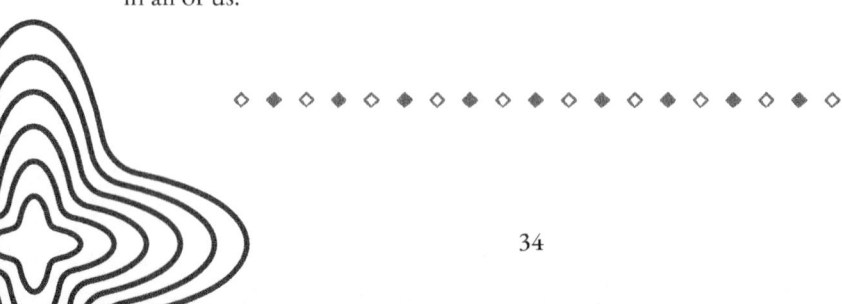

19

Say What You Really Think (Online or In Print)

You've experienced life, and with that comes a wealth of opinions that deserve to be shared. Don't hold back, express yourself boldly. Start a blog or carve out a space for yourself on Medium. Consider penning a provocative op-ed for your local newspaper. Whether you choose to rant, reflect, or rebel, make your voice heard not to incite arguments, but to provoke thought and awaken consciousness. If you aspire to cultivate an audience around your ideas, Substack could be your platform of choice. When you create your newsletter, give it a title that resonates powerfully, something like The Sage With the Side-Eye or Retired and Unfiltered. Embrace the idea that there's nothing more defiant than delivering raw truths from someone who has lived through the highs and lows, someone who has truly earned the right to speak. Your voice is an asset; use it to challenge the status quo and inspire others to think critically about the world around them.

20

Get Back Into a Mosh Pit or Dance Floor

Forget about having perfect cartilage for a solid headbang. Just search for your favorite band or their contemporary version, and secure those tickets. Utilize platforms like Bandsintown or Songkick to find out when they're performing next. Regardless of whether you're into punk, jazz, or funk, immerse yourself in the crowd. Let the energy of the venue absorb you. Move your body, jump, and don't second-guess the sweat that comes from letting loose. Allow the bass to resonate in your chest as you belt out the chorus with all the enthusiasm you had at 22. Concerts are not just for the young; they are for anyone who craves the experience of live music and connection. You're not too old for concerts; you are too alive to pass them up. Reclaim that exhilaration, stand among fellow enthusiasts, and enjoy the music that makes your spirit soar. It's time to awaken the rock star within and relish the freedom of the moment.

21

Do a Cold Plunge and Brag About It Loudly

Cold plunges transcend the realm of TikTok wellness influencers; they are a powerful practice that invigorates both the body and mind. Engaging in cold exposure builds resilience and fosters an unyielding spirit. The sheer act of immersing oneself in frigid water generates a rebellious energy that few experiences can match. To incorporate this revitalizing practice into your routine, seek out a spa that provides contrast therapy, combining the invigorating cold plunge with the soothing heat of a sauna. Alternatively, consider constructing a DIY cold plunge in your own backyard using a horse trough or stock tank—yes, it's not only practical but quite effective as well! Resources like Wim Hof's techniques can guide you on your journey, helping you harness the benefits of this exhilarating experience. The results will be nothing short of transformative: not only will your energy levels soar, but your neighbors will inevitably start to wonder, "What's that guy up to? Why does he look a decade younger?"

22

Challenge a Much Younger Man to a Game and Win

Choose your arena: Whether it's ping pong, pool, chess, cornhole, fantasy football, poker, or even Mario Kart, pick what excites you the most. The objective isn't necessarily to crush your rival, although if you happen to do so, that's certainly a bonus. This is more about reigniting the competitive spirit within you. Whether you're at the local rec center or hosting a challenge in your backyard, it's time to step up your game. Show no mercy and offer no apologies; this is the time to reclaim your throne. Raise the stakes by wagering a round of drinks or bragging rights. Let those younger challengers know that the seasoned warrior still knows how to play the game and has tricks up his sleeve. Remind everyone that experience is a powerful ally, and every move counts. So gather your friends, pick your battleground, and get ready to showcase your skills. The competition is fierce, and it's your time to shine.

23

Join or Start a Local "Men's Mischief Club"

Forget the cookie-cutter retiree clubs that suggest a quiet life of golf and bingo. What you really need is a crew that embodies the spirit of adventure and mischief. Gather a few like-minded guys who aren't ready to kick back and settle into a mundane routine. These are the men who crave excitement, meaningful connections, and the occasional cigar-fueled debate over life's deeper questions. Organize monthly "missions" that take you out of your comfort zone—think escape rooms that challenge your wits, paintball outings that unleash your competitive side, whiskey tastings that elevate your palate, or even charity pranks that give back while keeping things lively. Tap into your local community by using platforms like Nextdoor or Facebook Groups to recruit other spirited souls. Design custom T-shirts for your adventures and choose a humorous name that reflects your rebellious nature, like *The Rewired Brotherhood* or *Men of Mayhem (With Bad Knees)*. This is your tribe, your crew, a vibrant reminder that the urge to be wild and adventurous never truly fades.

Do That Thing They Said You Couldn't

What's the challenge someone once laid at your feet, insisting you couldn't tackle it? Perhaps it was running a 5K, launching a band, picking up French, or even growing your hair out long. That doubt still ignites a fire within you, doesn't it? Embrace that spark. Take the initiative and make it happen—not to simply defy their skepticism, but to validate your own potential. Dive into resources that empower you, like using apps such as Duolingo for language learning, enrolling in a "Couch to 5K" program to get fit, or dusting off that neglected Stratocaster to reignite your musical passions. There's nothing more rebellious than defying and exceeding expectations, especially those you've set for yourself. Each step you take toward that goal fuels your confidence and enhances your determination. So, harness that energy, channel your frustration, and turn it into motivation. Make your comeback—not for anyone else, but for the hero you strive to be. It's time to rise and show the world what you're truly capable of achieving.

Dave: The Dad Who Hung Up the Briefcase and Laced Up His Skates

Dave had barely been retired a week when the walls started closing in.

Not literally—his mortgage-free suburban home was standing just fine. But emotionally? Existentially? The man was pacing around like a Roomba with no clear destination. For 35 years, Dave had been the guy in the corner office with the tie slightly loosened and a black coffee permanently attached to his right hand. He led meetings, solved problems, and kept a family of six running smoother than his department's printer (which wasn't saying much).

Now? The house was quiet. *Too* quiet.

His four kids were grown, launched, and scattered across time zones. The house no longer echoed with slammed doors, sibling debates about who finished the orange juice, or the thump of a rogue soccer ball bouncing down the hallway. His wife had her yoga and book club routines. His calendar? A bleak white wasteland. Just blank boxes and the occasional "oil change" reminder.

He tried easing into it like all the "Top 10 Things to Do in Retirement" blogs suggested. Sat in the recliner. Read the paper cover to cover, even the obits. Watched squirrels. Tried organizing the garage. Twice. On day six, he dramatically sighed every time his wife asked what he wanted for lunch, like a Shakespearean character pondering whether turkey or ham was the meaning of life.

It wasn't depression exactly—it was more like the itchiness of the soul.

Dave had always known his retirement wouldn't look like his dad's. His old man had been a cardigan-wearing crossword puzzle ninja who could spend three hours debating the ethics of Mulligans on a golf course. But Dave? He didn't golf, and he didn't particularly enjoy watching sports either.

But playing them? That was different. That lit something up.

He still remembered how fast his heart beat under stadium lights back in high school hockey. The scent of the rink, the clatter of sticks, the cold air slicing across his face—it was pure adrenaline. He hadn't thought about that feeling in decades.

That night, fueled by mild boredom and a second glass of Merlot, Dave typed: "Men's hockey league 55+ near me."

Boom. Jackpot. A local community rink hosted a casual Monday night pick-up league. No tryouts. No egos. Just a bunch of guys with sore backs, bad knees, and unshakable nostalgia for the good ol' days.

Signing up was the easy part.

Stepping onto the ice for the first time in 30+ years? Terrifying.

His skates felt like medieval torture devices. His ankles wobbled like a newborn deer. His stickhandling was more "slapstick comedy" than "slap shot." But something magical happened between gasping for air and fumbling a pass to a guy named Roy who used to be a pediatric dentist: he started to feel alive again.

Each week, he got a little stronger. His legs stopped trembling. His instincts kicked in. The locker room became his new happy place—a mix of icy banter, dad jokes, and the kind of genuine camaraderie you can't fake. One guy brought beer. Another brought a Bluetooth speaker and only played 80s hair metal. They called themselves "The Silver Blades," half-joking, half-serious.

Six months in, Dave was hooked. He dropped 10 pounds without even trying. His blood pressure improved. His stress? Practically vanished. And for the first time in years, he had something to look forward to every week. Monday nights weren't the beginning of a workweek anymore. They were game night. They were his night.

Even his kids were impressed. "Wait—you're playing hockey again?" they asked, half in awe, half in horror.

"Damn right I am," Dave grinned, lacing up his skates with that twinkle he used to reserve for playoff season.

These days, Dave isn't talking about slowing down. He's debating switching to a composite stick and trying slap shots again. He even got his grandkids mini sticks and built a mini rink in the backyard for them.

Because retirement wasn't the end of his story.

It just meant turning the page, and this new chapter? Yeah, it's on ice. And Dave's not just skating. He's flying.

Final Thoughts: Rock On, Rebel King

Look at you—still standing, still dreaming, still turning heads.

If you've made it through this chapter, chances are something in you just woke up. That spark you thought had fizzled? Yeah, it's doing cartwheels now. Whether you're jamming with a local band, getting that tattoo, or finally telling people *exactly* what you think about pineapple on pizza, this chapter was all about reclaiming your edge. And guess what? The edge suits you.

But we're not done yet, King. Not even close.

Because next up, we're trading rebellion for adrenaline. The kind of travel that requires guts, grit, and maybe a few GoPro batteries. The kind that makes your kids say, "Wait, you did *what*?"

So, lace up those boots and grab your passport.

You've rebelled like a rockstar.

Now, it's time to travel like a legend.

Let's go.

CHAPTER 3

EXTREME TRAVEL ADVENTURES FOR THE RETIRED KING

This chapter is not for the faint of heart or those allergic to wind in their hair and stories that start with "So there I was, clinging to the edge of a volcano..." It's for the King who's swapped office chairs for skydiving gear, and spreadsheets for surfboards. If you've ever felt the itch for adventure but were told to "act your age," consider this your official permission slip to laugh in the face of that nonsense.

From zip lining through Costa Rican rainforests to ice-climbing in Banff, we're diving into the bold, the bucket list-worthy, and the "Wait, you really did that?" kind of travel. And no, you don't need to be 25 or own six-pack abs to join the club—you just need a solid sense of humor, a spark of curiosity, and the willingness to say *yes* a little more often.

We'll even go over some real-world spots where you can go from *hmm* to *heck yes* without breaking the bank or your hip. So buckle up, brave soul. The world is wide, wild, and waiting.

Let's go raise some eyebrows, and maybe your heart rate.

25

HELI-SKI THE BACKCOUNTRY OF BRITISH COLUMBIA

Forget about those manicured slopes and the soul-crushing long lift lines. Instead, consider booking a heli-skiing adventure where the only tracks in the pristine powder are yours and yours alone. Imagine being dropped by helicopter onto untouched terrain—it's like stepping onto a blanket of white velvet that extends as far as the eye can see. When it comes to operators, you can't go wrong with well-respected names like CMH Heli-Skiing or Bella Coola Heli Sports. Don't worry, you don't need to be the next Olympic champion to enjoy this experience; just be moderately fit and ready to face a thrill. After an exhilarating day of carving your own path on the slopes, you'll retreat to luxurious lodges where the amenities are as rich as the meals—think feasting like royalty every night. This isn't just skiing; it's a lifestyle reborn at dizzying heights. Retirement goal: making snow angels at a breathtaking 9,000 feet, fully embracing the winter wonderland.

26

Drive a Supercar on Germany's Autobahn

What perfectly conveys "I refuse to hit the brakes"? Zooming at a blistering 180 mph in a sleek Ferrari on the famed Autobahn. With companies like Porsche Drive and Ultimate Drives, you can take the wheel of high-performance machines, unleashing their power over miles of unrestricted road, all while following the law. Picture this: darting between picturesque towns, soaking in the breathtaking vistas of the Black Forest, and then pulling up to a cozy eatery to savor schnitzel paired with a refreshing beer. And as you enjoy that delicious meal, your smile screams, "I'm still the speed demon!" Let's face it, you weren't crafted for the mundane crawl of cruise control; you were built for the thrill of the fast lane, where the only speed limit is your own adventurous spirit. So, strap in and hit the gas, because life's too short for anything less than a high-octane ride.

27

Hike to Everest Base Camp

Mount Everest is often heralded as the pinnacle of aspiration, but let's not kid ourselves: just making it to Base Camp at a jaw-dropping 17,598 feet is a victory in its own right. It's not merely a trek; it's a physical challenge that pushes your limits, a mental exercise that sharpens your resolve, and a spiritual experience that can leave you humbled in the best possible way. The truth is, you don't even need to plant your flag atop the summit to earn your stripes. Simply being in the very spot where legends once roamed holds its own swagger. If you're not quite ready to tackle the heights solo, consider joining a reputable outfit like Intrepid Travel or G Adventures. They cater to the seasoned adventurers, offering leisurely-paced journeys that won't leave you gasping for breath. But be warned: Upon your return, you might find yourself donning prayer beads and referring to yourself as "Mountain Man," much to the amusement of your friends.

28

CAGE DIVE WITH GREAT WHITE SHARKS IN SOUTH AFRICA

You're not just comfortable in the deep end; you *own* it. So, why not take a leap—literally—into the waters of Gansbaai, South Africa, where the thrill of a shark-cage dive awaits? Imagine this: your adrenaline pumping, heart racing like it's auditioning for a role in an action flick. Operators like Marine Dynamics ensure your safety while maintaining an eco-conscious approach to this exhilarating experience. No prior diving experience? No problem! Just bring your unshakeable courage, boundless curiosity, and, of course, a trusty camera. You'll want to capture that moment for posterity—think of a new dating profile picture with the caption "Chillin' with Jaws." Who will be the apex predator on this adventure? Spoiler alert: you! It's time to swap ordinary weekends for the extraordinary, so plunge into the thrill, experience nature's raw power up close, and let the ocean's most formidable creature remind you just how alive you really are!

29

Motorcycle Across the Himalayas

Adventure reaches a whole new level of badassery when you throw a Royal Enfield into the mix, tearing through the world's loftiest roads like a modern-day knight on a metal steed. Feel the rush as you cruise through the spectacular landscapes of Leh, shimmy around the exhilarating curves of Manali, or plunge into the exotic allure of Bhutan's untamed trails, where every twist and turn offers views that would make even the most hardened traveler pause in awe. Companies such as Vintage Rides and Himalayan Motorbike Tours have your back, organizing epic group excursions led by local wizards of the road, complete with support vehicles carrying your gear. Picture this: dodging yaks as they nonchalantly block the road, tackling narrow mountain passes that seem to flirt with danger, and enjoying a well-earned cup of tea in serene monasteries, where the monks look at your handlebar mustache with a mixture of admiration and bewilderment. Spiritual *and* savage? That's the very essence of a retired king on two wheels.

30

Zip Line Through the Cloud Forest in Costa Rica

Just imagine soaring above the vibrant treetops at a heart-pounding 60 mph, with the playful screeches of monkeys echoing in the background as the cool mist kisses your cheeks. Welcome to Monteverde, where adventure awaits at every turn. The zip line parks, particularly the renowned Sky Adventures, boast some of the longest and highest zip lines on the globe. Among these adrenaline-pumping rides is the legendary Superman cable, which lets you fly through the air like the hero you were always meant to be. But wait, there's more! They've got hanging bridges that sway like a scene out of an action flick, and Tarzan swings that will have you channeling your inner jungle king. It's like stepping into your very own blockbuster movie, with you as the star of the show. And let's be honest, retirement is the ultimate excuse to embrace that weightless feeling—both literally as you zip through the air and figuratively as you leave the daily grind behind. Get ready for the thrill of a lifetime!

31

CROSS A DESERT ON CAMELBACK (LAWRENCE OF ARABIA-STYLE)

Forget the cruise buffet's mediocrity and gear up for a wild adventure that traces back to the roots of exploration. Picture yourself traversing the breathtaking expanse of the Wadi Rum desert in Jordan or the sweeping sands of the Sahara in Morocco, with seasoned Bedouin guides leading the charge on camelback. This isn't just any ordinary trip; it's a chance to immerse yourself in an age-old thrill that few have the guts to embrace. As the sun sets, you'll pitch your tent beneath the vast, twinkling sky, where the stars seem to wink at your daring spirit. Feast on a tantalizing fire-cooked tagine—because who needs fancy dining when you can savor authentic flavors alongside a crackling fire? And if you rise early enough, you'll witness the magnificent dunes blush crimson at dawn's first light. Organizations like Intrepid and Sahara Desert Crew handle all the nitty-gritty details. All you need is a sprinkle of grit, a stylish scarf, and a healthy dose of humor for when your camel decides it's time to sass back. It's not just a journey; it's an act of spiritual rebellion against the mundane.

32

Swim With Manta Rays at Night in Hawaii

If glowing oceans and otherworldly sea creatures don't scream *vibrant*, then what on earth does? Embark on a nighttime manta ray dive or snorkel excursion on the breathtaking Big Island of Hawaii with fantastic operators like Manta Ray Dives of Hawaii. You'll find yourself gliding beneath floodlights, surrounded by these colossal, gentle giants as they perform their mesmerizing underwater acrobatics. Imagine being transported inside a living sci-fi movie—except, instead of anxiously binge-watching on Netflix, you're fully engaged, serene, and in awe of the awe-inspiring wonders of nature. This underwater experience is pure magic, available only to those daring enough to embrace it. You'll be treated to a natural spectacle that tantalizes all your senses, a thrilling journey that invites you to leave the ordinary behind. So grab your snorkel gear, muster your courage, and prepare yourself for a night like no other, where the ocean floor becomes a stage and you, my friend, are the captivated audience.

33

Trek Through Patagonia With Nothing But a Pack and a Plan

The southern tip of South America is like nature's own amusement park, complete with wild landscapes, glaciers that look like they've been sculpted by a master artist, and cliffs that seem to challenge the very concept of gravity. Picture yourself in the breathtaking national parks of Torres del Paine in Chile or El Chaltén in Argentina, where the trails are as world-class as they come. Now, you can either tag along with a reliable company like Swoop Patagonia or throw on your backpack and channel your inner adventurer with a little DIY spirit. You don't need to be the next Bear Grylls to tackle these paths—just bring some determination and a willingness to embrace the unexpected. Make sure to pack layers for those unpredictable weather swings, and don't forget your trekking poles; they'll be your best friends. Oh, and a good dose of rugged humor is essential—because who doesn't need a laugh while conquering the great outdoors? Let the trail be your therapist, turning this adventure into nothing short of a personal transformation.

34

Volcano Boarding in Nicaragua

Absolutely. You read that correctly. Picture this: you're actually climbing an active volcano—Cerro Negro—and then, without a second thought, you're hurtling down its steep, black gravel slopes like a snowless snowboarder with all the rebellious flair of a rock star. This adrenaline-pumping escapade is exclusively found in León, Nicaragua, courtesy of adventurous groups like Bigfoot Hostel & Volcano Boarding. It's a whirlwind of excitement that's over in a flash but leaves lasting impressions that you won't soon forget. Fair warning: You'll need goggles to protect those peepers, a fair dose of guts to tackle the wild ride, and—let's not forget—just the right amount of swagger to pull it all off. Who said retirement had to be dull? Forget about sipping tea on the porch; this is the kind of thrill that injects life into your years and keeps the spirit of adventure alive. Forget mundane; let's make memories that are reckless and downright fun!

35

Skydive Over the Swiss Alps

Craving the pinnacle of thrill-seeking? Take a leap from a plane and soar over the breathtaking landscapes of Interlaken, Switzerland. With Skydive Interlaken, you'll find yourself in a thrilling freefall, zipping past majestic glaciers, towering mountain peaks, and shimmering turquoise lakes that take your breath away. This isn't just a skydive; it's an exhilarating experience that lands squarely on any self-respecting adventurer's bucket list. The thrill? Absolutely electrifying. The photographs you'll snag? Unquestionably heroic. And that's not all—once you've conquered the skies and your adrenaline is still racing, you can saunter over to a quaint alpine lodge to indulge in some well-deserved schnapps and fondue. Picture yourself with a cozy mug in one hand and a plate of gooey cheese in the other, swapping tales of your aerial escapades. You'll be the master of mixing modesty with just the right amount of bravado, armed with unforgettable *sky stories* that will leave your friends green with envy.

36

Sail the Greek Islands Like a Pirate King

Swap those land legs for sea legs and set sail on an unforgettable adventure through the enchanting Greek Isles aboard a sailboat or catamaran. You can easily charter your own trusty floating vessel via platforms like Sailo or G Adventures Sailing Tours. Once you're out there, take the plunge and dive off the deck into the mesmerizing sapphire waters that shimmer like jewels under the sun. You'll have the chance to dock at secluded coves that are often overlooked by the average traveler. Enjoy a glass of ouzo while basking under a blanket of stars, letting the gentle lapping of the waves serenade you into bliss. Whether you choose to take the helm yourself or hand over the reins to a seasoned captain, know that you're not just a passenger; you're the ruler of your own maritime kingdom. Bonus points if you rock some linen attire, cultivate a distinguished salt-and-pepper beard, and strut your stuff as "The Captain" for the week. Your legendary status awaits!

37

Ice Climb a Frozen Waterfall in Iceland

Regular climbing is undoubtedly a thrill, but let's talk about *ice* climbing—now that's a whole new ballpark of excitement! Imagine standing before towering, frozen vertical walls that shimmer with a stunning blue hue, practically begging for you to give them a go. If you're looking to tap into your inner adventurer, Iceland is the place to unleash that wild spirit. Team up with the legends over at Arctic Adventures or Icelandic Mountain Guides, and they'll provide everything you need to get started, from crampons and ice axes to comprehensive safety training. No experience? No problem! Just make sure your knees are up for the challenge and that you have a craving for the extraordinary. And here's the cherry on top: Once you've conquered those icy giants, you can kick back and unwind in the iconic Blue Lagoon with a cold beer in hand. You'll emerge feeling like a Norse god, having transformed winter into your personal playground.

38

CROSS THE ARCTIC CIRCLE ON A DOG SLED

If snowmobiles feel a tad too timid and cruises lean heavily on the cozy side, how about embracing a heart-racing expedition where you're towed across the vast, icy expanse of the Arctic tundra by a pack of formidable, howling huskies? Picture yourself mushing through the breathtaking realms of northern Finland or Norway, guided by the experts from Tromsø Villmarkssenter or Harriniva. Spend your nights in a secluded cabin, cuddled up with the warmth of the dogs, as you chase the mesmerizing northern lights dancing across the sky. In the morning, you'll wake up with a furry companion nestled beside your sleeping bag—blissfully rugged, exhilarating, and surprisingly serene. It's an act of defiance against the mundane noise, the cushy comfort zones, and the monotonous, slow pace of everyday life. You're not merely slapping on a tourist sticker; you're fully immersed in the art of sled-legending, carving your own adventure on the frigid canvas of the Arctic wilderness.

Dive Between Two Continents in Silfra Fissure, Iceland

Where can you honestly swim between tectonic plates, you ask? Look no further than Iceland—once again, the rebellious rock star of the globe. At Silfra, you have the audacious opportunity to scuba dive or snorkel in the stunningly clear waters of glacial melt, right between the North American and Eurasian tectonic plates. Imagine this: a visibility of 100 meters, so pristine that it feels like you're diving in a movie set. Companies like Dive.is have your back, providing dry suits and all the gear you need to dive headfirst into this geological playground. You'll drift through an underwater canyon that feels akin to nature giving you a high-five—talk about a warm welcome! Science? Absolutely. Adventure? You bet your bottom dollar. And bragging rights? They're as secure as a locked vault. This surreal experience is bound to make you ponder, "Why on Earth did I wait so long to embrace this epic slice of life?" Dive in, my friend; the adventure is calling!

How Harold Reclaimed His Wild Side in the Arctic Circle

At 68, freshly retired Harold Jenkins felt less like a free man and more like a well-kept houseplant—fed, watered, and slowly withering. Retirement, once a dream, quickly turned into oatmeal breakfasts, local news, and Home Depot strolls. Even his daughters' gift— a "King of the Couch" blanket—started to itch with irony.

Harold didn't want comfort. He wanted stories. The kind that began with "So there I was…" and ended in disbelief.

One cold morning, on a whim (and a caffeine kick), he googled "Crazy adventures for retirees." The winner? Dog sledding across the Arctic Circle in Norway.

Two weeks later, Harold found himself wrapped in thermal gear, clutching a sled as six wild-eyed huskies—Thor, Blizzard, Noodle, Fang, Skippy, and Denise—bounced with anticipation. After a two-minute crash course, he was off. Chaos reigned at first: dogs pooped, he screamed, the sled nearly flipped, but Harold held on.

And then—he laughed. Really laughed. The kind of laugh that shakes off decades of expectations.

By day three, he knew the dogs by name, whispered encouragement through snowstorms, and let Denise sleep on his legs. He drank mystery stews, stared at firelight, and gasped at northern lights like they were just for him. His back ached. His soul didn't.

Back home, the grandkids didn't care about his engineering days—they wanted to hear about the huskies, the storm, and the snow faceplant. They made him a new fleece blanket: "Grandpa Glacier."

The old one? Donated.

Because Harold discovered something most people forget: You don't retire from adventure. You retire *into* it.

Final Thoughts: Adventure Isn't a Phase—It's a Lifestyle

So, here's the truth: You didn't just read a chapter, you cracked open a treasure chest of adrenaline. Whether you're zip lining in Ecuador, chasing the Northern Lights in Iceland, or finally taking that motorcycle road trip across Route 66, you've officially proven that retirement isn't about slowing down—it's about leveling up.

And the best part? You're not done yet.

You've faced the mountains, the waves, the skies. Now it's time to face something just as exhilarating: other people. (Cue dramatic music.) But seriously—while solo thrills are epic, nothing beats a deep belly laugh with a good friend, a spontaneous dance at a summer street fair, or sharing a bottle of wine with strangers-turned-buddies on a food tour in Tuscany.

Next up? We're diving into social adventures—the kind that spark connection, laughter, and maybe even a bromance or two. Think dinner parties with flair, travel clubs with soul, and hobbies that turn into lifelong friendships.

Because being King isn't just about conquering mountains—it's about building your kingdom.

Let's go find your people.

CHAPTER 4

FRIENDS, FUN, AND FRESH STARTS—SOCIAL ADVENTURES THAT SPARK JOY AND CONNECTION

Let's face it—skydiving is great, but laughing until you cry over fish tacos with your oldest friends? That's the good stuff.

Sure, adventures that spike your heart rate are thrilling, but adventures that fill your heart? Those are unforgettable. In this chapter, we're trading in hiking boots for happy hours, flight goggles for poker chips, and solo missions for social magic. Because the truth is, retirement is the perfect time to refresh your social circle, reconnect with your old crew, or even build an entirely new band of brothers (and sisters) to roll with.

Maybe you've lost touch with your college roommate. Maybe you're tired of surface-level small talk. Or maybe, just maybe, you're wondering if there's more to life than gardening in silence (no offense to tomatoes). Good news: there is.

We're diving into dinner clubs, pub trivia nights, laughter yoga (yes, it's a thing), group travel, community theater, local festivals, and backyard BBQs that turn into summer traditions. We'll even drop real places, websites, and apps that make showing up socially way easier than it used to be.

This isn't about being popular—it's about being plugged in. So pull up a chair, pour yourself a drink, and get ready to say "yes" to new people, new laughs, and a whole new way of showing up in the world.

Because real joy? It's best when shared.

Let's get social, Your Majesty.

Host a Backyard Film Night: Popcorn and Personality Required

Elevate your yard, balcony, or rooftop into the ultimate outdoor theater that will make the whole neighborhood green with envy. You don't need a Hollywood budget; a projector (check Amazon for options under $100) will do the trick. Stretch out a white sheet for a screen, set up a few lawn chairs, and curate a lineup of your favorite cult classics that'll have everyone quoting lines long after the credits roll. Spread the word by posting invites on Nextdoor or Meetup, and why not sprinkle in a quirky theme? How about "Totally Tubular '80s Night," "Action Heroes & Nachos," or "BYOB & Cringe-Worthy Rom-Coms"? And here's a clever twist: Let your guests vote on the next movie to keep things interesting. It's a creative and laid-back way to bask under the stars while forging new friendships between films and laughter. You provide the movies; they'll ensure it's a night to remember.

41

Join an Improv Class Even if You Think You're Not Funny

The quickest way to forge those connections? Share a good laugh. Improv is essentially social rocket fuel, propelling you out of your comfort zone and nudging you to embrace absurd ideas. Imagine bonding with total strangers over ridiculously funny scenes and epic flops. It's like comedy boot camp, only without the sweat and with a lot more joy. Check out classes at The Second City, your local community theater, or search for "Improv for Beginners" on Meetup. Remember, it's not about putting on a show; it's all about being present in the moment and letting the hilarity unfold. You'll stroll in with the classic apprehensive thought of "What the heck am I doing here?" and waltz out with a band of new pals and a treasure trove of inside jokes. The beauty of improv lies in its spontaneity; you'll find that laughter truly is the best glue for building friendships. So take the plunge; your funny bone will thank you!

42

Organize a Monthly "Mystery Meetup" Group

Round up a handful of your most curious friends and embark on an exhilarating monthly escapade—but the kicker? Only the host is privy to the grand scheme. Imagine the excitement: One month you might find yourselves hurling axes like lumberjacks, all in good fun, and the next, you could be doing yoga with goats in a tranquil farm setting. A private group chat or an email list is your best bet for organizing these outings and establishing a price limit that suits everyone's budget. The beauty of this arrangement lies in the fact that everyone will take turns hosting, infusing each event with their unique flair and creativity. It's a delightful mix of spontaneity and imagination that keeps everyone on their toes. No one ever knows what thrilling adventure awaits, but they can rest assured it's bound to be a blast. That shared experience of eager anticipation is the kind of bonding that transforms mere acquaintances into fast friends, sealing connections with a touch of thrilling suspense.

43

START A HOBBY SWAP NIGHT

Possess a unique skill? Don't keep it under wraps—let it shine! Looking to dive into something new? Then make the effort to show up! Organize an evening where you and a handful of like-minded individuals can exchange knowledge. Whether it's wood carving, calligraphy, the fine art of sourdough baking, or even harmonica playing, the sky's the limit! Imagine this as a fusion of adult show-and-tell and a TEDx talk, all taking place in the comfort of your garage. Pack up your tools, gather some tasty snacks, and arm yourself with an overwhelming sense of curiosity. The only stipulation is to share something that truly ignites your passion. You'll encounter fellow enthusiasts who share your quirks and obsessions, and that's where the magic happens! It's all about fostering genuine connections and discovering that you're not alone in your weird and wonderful interests. So go ahead, bring your talents to the table, and enjoy a night of enlightening exchanges and vibrant camaraderie!

44

Join a Community Art Project or Mural Team

Art possesses an enchanting ability to forge connections among strangers, much like an unexpected bond formed over a shared love for pineapple on pizza—controversial yet oddly satisfying. Whether you're getting involved in a vibrant group mural, a bold community sculpture, or a whimsical collaborative paint-by-numbers installation, diving into a community art project allows you to unleash your creativity. Additionally, it pairs well with the delightful experience of making friends with those brave enough to embrace the delightful chaos of paint splatters and mixed media mayhem. Keep your eyes peeled for opportunities at your local art centers, check out VolunteerMatch for nearby gigs, or tap into your city's arts council for some fun adventures. And let's not forget the added bonus: You'll be leaving a literal mark on your community. Plus, expect to receive a few paint-splattered high-fives along the way as you mingle with fellow art enthusiasts who appreciate the beauty of artistic expression, messy hands and all!

45

Host a Themed Potluck with a Twist

Food has an uncanny talent for uniting folks, but when you toss in some peculiar hats, you've got a recipe for an unforgettable gathering. Pick a whimsical theme—think "Nostalgic Comfort Food" or "Life-Altering Meals"—and invite your guests to bring along a dish paired with a quirky hat. The hat serves as the perfect icebreaker, sparking laughter and stories, while the meal stirs up memories and hearty laughter. To elevate the fun, introduce some lighthearted awards like "Most Mysterious Dish," where everyone wonders what on earth it could be, or "Best Hat Backstory," giving a nod to the tales behind those outrageous headpieces. This isn't merely another dinner party; it's an extraordinary experience of culinary joy, boundless creativity, and a delightful reminder not to take life too seriously. Picture the smiles, the laughter, and the shared memories—all wrapped up in the delicious flavors of your guests' cherished recipes and their laughable hats. It's a celebration of life, food, and the sheer joy of whimsy.

46

Take a Dance Class With a Social Spin

Whether you're getting your groove on with salsa or making a conga line out of life itself, partner-style dance classes are the ultimate playground for connection. Think about it—every time the next song kicks in, it's like a speed dating event, but with more rhythm and less awkward small talk. You'll be twirling and shimmying with a fresh partner every few minutes, which means you're on your way to meeting at least a dozen new faces in just one night. Keep your eyes peeled for beginner-friendly classes at local community centers, our pals at DanceTonight, or even those adult learning programs. Trust me, you'll fumble through steps together, share a good laugh about it, and who knows? You might just stumble upon someone who's down for a post-class beer. Plus, here's the cherry on top: After this, you'll never be that poor soul sitting out at weddings while everyone else is tearing up the dance floor.

47

HOST A GAME NIGHT BUT MAKE IT OFFBEAT

Forget about Monopoly; it's time to kick it up a notch! Think Cards Against Humanity, Code Names, or set up an epic DIY scavenger hunt that'll have everyone running around like kids again. Don't stop there—how about diving into some retro video games? Yes, I'm talking about Mario Kart tournaments that'll get your competitive spirit roaring! Or, why not bring the Olympic spirit to your backyard with a hilarious twist? Picture this: speed Jenga, where every second counts, adult hopscotch that takes you back to your childhood but with a refreshing drink in hand, and karaoke roulette, where everyone rolls the dice on their vocal talents! Send out the invites to neighbors, old colleagues, or random folks from Meetup. Remember, the sillier, the better—joyful chaos is the name of the game! Before you know it, a few games and a couple of drinks later, you'll find yourself in a circle of people who feel more like family than just acquaintances.

48

Start a Story Circle or "Five-Minute Tales" Night

Here's a little nugget of wisdom for you: Nearly everyone craves attention, and let's be honest, we all have a penchant for a captivating tale. So, gather around, my friends! Round up a group of six to eight brave souls willing to take a plunge into the vault of their memories and regale the rest of us with a short, true story from their fabulous lives—whether it's hilarious, impactful, or simply jaw-dropping. Set the stage with a five-minute timer to keep things spirited. No need to stress about the spotlight; think of it as a lighthearted storytelling therapy session, perhaps with a glass of wine to loosen those storytelling chops. Change it up by rotating hosts with each round. You could spice things up with fun themes like "Worst Job Ever," "First Big Adventure," or "Unexpected Hero." Trust me, you'll transcend from mere acquaintances to deep, soul-connected amigos by the end of the night—just like that!

Go on a "Stranger Mission" at a Local Festival or Market

Rally your crew or embrace your inner lone wolf as you embark on an adventure to a street fair, farmer's market, or vibrant cultural festival. Here's the challenge: Approach five strangers and extract a nugget of wisdom or amusement from each interaction. It could be anything from an intriguing recipe, perhaps a secret ingredient that will elevate your kitchen game, to a hilarious joke that could serve as your new go-to icebreaker. Maybe you'll stumble upon a recommendation for a local band that will become your next obsession, or even receive a slice of life advice that could steer your ship in a new direction. Don't forget to bring along a trusty notebook or whip out your phone for some selfies with your newfound companions. This isn't just a casual outing; it's the fine art of low-stakes connection, where each booth presents a new opportunity, and every chat holds the potential to become an unforgettable story. Embrace the thrill of the unknown!

50

Sign Up for a Creative Retreat or Weekend Workshop

From songwriting retreats in the heart of Nashville to pottery workshops nestled in the vibrant streets of Santa Fe, there's an entire universe filled with creative retreats designed specifically for adults eager to craft and connect. These experiences aren't just about honing your skills; they provide a unique opportunity to meet like-minded individuals who share your passion for creativity. Explore fantastic offerings from The Makerie, immerse yourself in the enriching programs of Road Scholar, or dive into the diverse adventures available through Airbnb Experiences. Whether you find yourself weaving intricate baskets or tapping into your literary flair while writing flash fiction, the essence of creativity fosters vibrant connections. There's something undeniably special about bonding with fellow creatives, especially when you're literally elbow-deep in clay, shaping your next masterpiece, or sharing infectious laughs over how hilariously bad your mandala turned out. So grab your apron, unleash your inner artist, and get ready to create lasting memories while crafting something extraordinary.

51

Volunteer for a Flash Mob or Performance Group

Yes, they absolutely still exist—and trust me, they're a riot! Some cities have these so-called "secret" dance flash mobs, spontaneous choir gatherings, or even improv performances that extend an open invitation to anyone daring enough to jump in after a bit of practice. Take a look at Flash Mob America or dive into Facebook to find flash mobs or public performance groups that are stirring things up in your neck of the woods. You'll engage in some rehearsals, share a few hearty laughs, and perhaps even find yourself blushing a bit in public—it's all part of the charm! In the end, you'll forge instant friendships because nothing quite brings people together like the delightful combination of shared absurdity, the joy of synchronized dance moves, and the occasional slip-up that leaves everyone in stitches. So, put on your dancing shoes and prepare for some unforgettable moments filled with rhythm, laughter, and camaraderie!

Frank Discovers the Unexpected Joy of Painting Mandalas (Badly) in Boulder

Frank Deluca was 72, proudly retired from a four-decade-long career as a financial advisor, and so logically minded that he once calculated the most efficient way to load a dishwasher—and printed a diagram for his grandchildren.

Creativity, to Frank, was organizing his sock drawer by both color and season. His idea of "flow" involved spreadsheets and quarterly projections. He was not, by any means, an "energy vortex" kind of guy. He believed in rational thinking, predictable outcomes, and not owning anything labeled boho.

But when his wife, Maria, passed away after 47 years of shared routines, Sunday dinners, and evening Jeopardy rituals, something in Frank… paused.

At first, he clung to structure like a life raft. Made perfectly balanced breakfasts. Reorganized the pantry alphabetically. Read four books on estate planning. But grief doesn't respect neat columns. It creeps in sideways, usually in the silence after dinner, or in the empty space on the left side of the bed.

Then one morning, he opened his email and saw a message from his daughter.

Subject line: Dad, don't delete this one. Inside was a link to The Makerie's Creative Retreat in Boulder, Colorado, with a note that read: "It's time to try something new, Dad. And no, Sudoku tournaments don't count."

Frank sighed. He muttered something about "hippies with paintbrushes." But he clicked the link. And then, perhaps out of boredom… perhaps out of something deeper… he signed up.

He packed three flannel shirts, emergency granola bars, and a healthy dose of skepticism.

When he arrived, he was greeted by an instructor named Skye, who was barefoot, wore six bangles on each wrist, and said things like, "We don't create with our hands—we create with our hearts." Frank made a mental note to sit in the back row.

The first class? Mandala Painting. Circles. Patterns. Colors. The kind of thing that gave Frank mild anxiety, because what's the ROI on a mandala?

But then something surprising happened.

He picked up a paintbrush.

His hands trembled slightly. His first circle was more of an aggressive oval. His pattern looked like a lopsided pizza. And he accidentally dipped his sleeve in purple paint, then spent the rest of the session looking like he had been tackled by a Muppet in the dark.

But he laughed. Not politely, either. He *really* laughed.

And the laughter... didn't stop.

The retreat was full of people from all walks of life: a retired opera singer, a school nurse who now makes candles for a living, a guy named Kevin who used to be a lawyer and now bakes gluten-free muffins for farmers' markets. They painted. They shared stories. They ate shockingly good vegetarian food. They cried a little. They belly-laughed a lot.

Frank wasn't the best painter—not by a long shot—but he started looking forward to each session. There was something deeply calming, almost meditative, about watching color fill a page with no agenda.

No numbers. No pressure. Just paint.

By the end of the weekend, Frank had painted three mandalas: each one more confident, more vibrant, and slightly less pizza-like than the last.

But more importantly, he walked away with something unexpected: connection. He left Boulder with a phone full of new contacts and a standing invite to a weekly Zoom call with some of his fellow "retreat rebels."

Now, every Tuesday evening, Frank joins Mandala and Merlot Night. He sets up his little corner table with a glass of red, some mellow jazz, and a blank canvas. They chat, they roast each other's abstract "masterpieces," and they remind each other that getting messy is part of the joy.

His daughter popped in on a Zoom once and nearly spat out her tea upon seeing her dad in an apron with paint on his nose, laughing at a joke about "chakra alignment."

Frank still uses spreadsheets. He still organizes his sock drawer.

But now he also paints. And he's added a new word to his vocabulary: *whimsy*.

He's even considering going back to Boulder next year—maybe for a fiber arts class. (He still doesn't quite know what that is, but he's oddly okay with that.)

Because what he's discovered—through crooked circles, watercolor explosions, and hilarious paint disasters—is that trying something new doesn't mean abandoning who you are.

It means expanding who you *can be*.

Final Thoughts: Your Royal Circle Is Just the Beginning

You came, you mingled, you made 'em laugh. Whether you reconnected with an old friend, joined a travel group, hosted your first themed dinner party, or finally said yes to salsa night—bravo, King. You didn't just expand your social calendar; you expanded your world.

Because connection isn't a luxury—it's lifeblood. It's the clinking of glasses, the shared glances of "Did we really just do that?", and the gentle nudge of someone saying, "Come with me, this'll be fun."

But here's the thing: Now that you've built a circle, it's time to test your edge.

The next chapter will move you out of your comfort zone and bring out your courage. It's for the moments that shake you, shape you, and leave you a little speechless in the best possible way. We're talking real-deal, mind-shifting, heart-pounding, legacy-level adventures.

So, dust off that dream you've been shelving. Pack curiosity, and bring your upgraded confidence.

Because next? We're not just having fun, we're becoming unforgettable.

Let's go build your legend.

CHAPTER 5

OUT OF THE COMFORT ZONE, INTO THE LEGEND—BOLD ADVENTURES THAT CHANGE YOU

There's nothing wrong with comfort. A cozy chair, a good book, a Sunday roast—delicious. But you didn't come all this way just to coast. You're not a man of "maybe someday." You're a man of now.

This chapter is about the kind of adventures that rearrange your soul. The bold moves that make you a little nervous, and a lot alive. Whether it's taking the stage at a local open mic, walking the Camino de Santiago, going on a solo sabbatical, or learning to dance in a city where you don't speak the language (yet), these are the stories you'll tell for the rest of your life.

They don't require you to be perfect, but they do require presence. And a willingness to step beyond what's familiar.

Because honestly, legends aren't born from comfort zones. They're forged in the fire of "holy crap, I'm actually doing this."

So, let's stop playing it safe.

Let's make retirement your origin story.

52

LEARN A LANGUAGE IN THE COUNTRY THAT SPEAKS IT

Forget the comfy couch and the lifeless Duolingo app; it's time to plunge headfirst into a real-life language extravaganza! Picture this: a two-week (or longer) language class in the sunny streets of Spain, the vibrant markets of Costa Rica, or the bustling cities of Japan, where your "homework" involves nothing less than ordering exquisite tapas or bartering at a lively street market. Programs like EF Language Travel or the delightful FluentU Immersion Retreats have it all—daily language lessons that ignite your skills, combined with cultural excursions that have you laughing, stumbling, and making memories that an ordinary classroom can't touch. You'll trip over words, crack up over your own blunders, and inevitably bond with locals over your hilarious language mishaps. And let's be honest: Nothing breaks the ice quite like a good language blooper. So, gear up for an adventure that's not just about learning a language; it's about diving into a world where every mistake is a conversation starter.

53

Go Whitewater Rafting on a Wild River

If you've never found yourself clinging to the side of a raft, yelling "LEFT PADDLE!" while surrounded by a bunch of strangers who are just as confused, are you even experiencing life in all its chaotic glory? Ditch the mundane and propel yourself into the exhilarating realm of class III or IV rapids with a legendary outfitter like OARS or NOC Adventures. Whether you choose to conquer the majestic Colorado River, tackle the wild waters of the Zambezi, or brave the tumultuous Ottawa, whitewater rafting is not just an adventure; it's a test of teamwork, trust, and an absolute demand for *total presence*. As you navigate those roaring waves, the adrenaline surges, and by the end of it all, you'll emerge utterly soaked, pleasantly sore, and sporting a grin that's more wildman than civilized human. And that memory—a roaring highlight reel etched in your brain? Oh, it's here to stay, a permanent badge of honor in the epic tale that is your life.

54

TRY ZERO-GRAVITY OR FLIGHT SIMULATION TRAINING

You might not be packing your bags for a Mars mission, but let's be honest—you can get pretty darn close to liftoff right here on Earth! Buckle up for the Zero G Experience, where you'll get your very own taste of what it's like to be in zero gravity, all thanks to a specially-modified Boeing 727. Forget the astronaut suit for a moment; this is where the real magic happens. If you're yearning for something that keeps your feet a tad closer to solid ground, how about trying your hand at jet pilot training or stepping into a Boeing flight simulator? Head on over to places like iFLY Jets, where you'll find an exhilarating mix of science fiction flair and Top Gun bravado. It's the perfect recipe for shaking up your daily routine and leaving your comfort zone behind. So, whether you're floating in zero G or soaring high in a simulator, prepare for an experience that's sure to send your adrenaline levels into orbit!

55

Live With a Local in Another Country for a Week

Forget about the cookie-cutter hotels that have all the charm of a cardboard box. Instead, dive into the rich tapestry of local life with homestays or community-based travel platforms like Workaway, Trusted Housesitters, or Couchsurfing. Picture this: You could be living in a quaint Balinese village, soaking up the sun and local customs. Ever fancied herding goats in New Zealand? That's right, take a break from the usual tourist routes and jump headfirst into the extraordinary. Or how about whipping up some pasta alongside a charming nonna in Sicily? It's not just a cooking lesson; it's a lifeline to authentic Italian culture. You'll be wearing many hats—part guest, part student, and all local. This experience goes far beyond sightseeing; it reshapes your understanding of "normal." Embrace the local culture, make new friends, and create unforgettable memories. Trust me, there's no better recipe for an adventure than jumping into the heart of a new place!

56

TAKE A WEEKLONG WILDERNESS SURVIVAL COURSE

Put away that shiny smartphone and embrace the wild! It's time to tap into your primal instincts by mastering the art of survival. Learn to conjure flames from mere sticks, construct a fortress out of natural materials, and differentiate between what's tasty and what'll send you running for the nearest hospital. Check out programs at Boulder Outdoor Survival School or Trackers Earth, where you'll be digging in the dirt and honing your skills like a true outdoorsman. By the end of your adventure, you'll be sporting some battle scars—think blisters from your impressive fire-starting skills and dirt embedded in your beard that tells tales of your rugged exploits. You'll emerge feeling as if you could navigate the wilderness with nothing but your wits—or at least handle a power outage with style. Comfort zones? What are those? They've got nothing on the thrill of embracing nature and testing your limits! So, pack your bags and get ready for a journey that'll redefine your idea of living!

57

LEARN TO CODE OR BUILD A MOBILE APP

It's not merely a playground for those fresh-faced 20-somethings in hoodies and sneakers. We've got platforms like Codeacademy and FreeCodeCamp that break down the mystical world of coding into bite-sized, digestible nuggets for mere mortals. Feel like flexing your creative muscles? Why not whip up an app to meticulously track your golf scores, build a slick website for your local chess aficionados, or finally, bring that dusty photo collection into the digital age? Sure, it may seem a bit nerdy, but let's be real—it's incredibly empowering. Think of it as sharpening your brain with the precision of a samurai sword, cutting through the fog of ignorance and uncertainty. You'll not only gain skills that dazzle friends at parties, but you'll also strut through life with the confidence of someone who knows their way around algorithms. Trust me, once you dive in, you might just find you've unearthed a hidden talent for tech wizardry that you never knew existed!

58

TRY URBAN EXPLORATION (A.K.A. URBEX ADVENTURES)

Dive into the exhilarating world of urban exploration, where abandoned buildings, derelict train stations, shadowy underground tunnels, and forgotten locales await your adventurous spirit—all while keeping it safe and legal, of course. Joining an urban explorer group is the ticket to experiences that many only dream of. Cities often host organized tours (just peek at Facebook or check out Atlas Obscura for the latest happenings). The thrill of stepping into a space where nature has started to reclaim its territory is equal parts eerie and enchanting, offering a strange beauty that's simply hard to resist. Before you embark on your journey, don't forget to pack the essentials: a trusty flashlight to pierce through the darkness, a camera to capture unrepeatable moments, and, most importantly, a sense of wonder to fully embrace the experience. Some of these locations will feel like time capsules, and you'll have the unique honor of being one of the few who gets to glimpse their hidden stories.

59

Train for and Run an Unusual Race

Ditch the dull 5Ks that feel like a slow march to boredom and dive headfirst into an offbeat race that'll keep you on your toes—and your taste buds tingling! Ever heard of the Krispy Kreme Challenge? Well, here's how it goes: you sprint, scarf down donuts, and then somehow manage to keep running. Yes, it's as gloriously messy as it sounds. Or how about embracing your inner warrior with the Savage Race? We're talking mud, fire, and a gauntlet of obstacles that'll have you questioning your life choices while simultaneously forging some epic tales of triumph. And let's not forget those vibrant color runs! You'll cross the finish line looking like a human canvas splattered with every hue imaginable, resembling a splendidly chaotic work of art. These races not only push you beyond your limits but also connect you with awesome people who share your zest for the absurd. Train hard, laugh harder, and enjoy the wild stories you'll share for years to come.

60

Do a "Fear Day" Once a Month

This might be a solo undertaking, but don't let that fool you: it packs a punch. Take a good look in the mirror and pick a fear that makes your stomach do somersaults—public speaking, awkward mingling at a party, or belting out a high note in front of an audience. Now, muster your courage and face it head-on. Create a shortlist of those fears that flirt with your limits, and then, like a true warrior, tackle one each month. Better yet, bring a buddy along for moral support; after all, misery loves company! Capture your brave moments on video—trust me, you'll want to relive these gems. And don't forget to throw yourself a mini-celebration for every courageous effort! Remember, being fearless isn't the point—it's about showing up and doing it regardless. Retirement isn't a shrinking of your world; it's an invitation to expand it, one audacious moment at a time. Embrace the adventure!

61

Learn to Sail So You Can Captain Your Own Damn Ship

You've been on the receiving end of orders long enough; it's high time you *send them sailing into the sunset*. Learning to sail is not merely a matter of mastering ropes, tying knots, and learning which way is starboard. No, my friend, it's about embracing freedom, boosting your confidence, and taking on the wild with style. Sure, the first time you step aboard, you might feel like you're stuck in a windstorm of confusion, trying to decipher tack, jibe, and wind direction from the ever-familiar *what the heck just happened?* But hang tight; before you know it, you'll be interpreting the water like it's Shakespeare. Consider enrolling in a beginner's course through the American Sailing Association or the RYA if you're across the pond. You have options: a weeklong liveaboard course in the Caribbean, a weekend crash course at your local marina, or a communal sailing adventure in Greece where you pick up skills as you explore. You'll encounter seasoned sailors, sun-drenched dreamers, and fellow thrill-seekers. Every gust of wind will feel like a congratulatory pat on the back from Mother Nature herself. And that glorious moment when you set off solo? That's when it hits you—you're not merely kicking back; you're *unshackled* and sailing into the great wide open.

62

GET SCUBA CERTIFIED BECAUSE THERE'S A WHOLE WORLD UNDERWATER WAITING FOR YOU

Land may be fantastic, but let's face it—70% of our planet is composed of water, and it's beckoning you. Learning to scuba dive is akin to unlocking a door to another universe. Picture yourself gliding effortlessly through vibrant coral cathedrals, catching a knowing glance from a wise sea turtle, and embracing a tranquility that no yoga retreat, no matter how zen, can ever replicate. Sure, you'll need some training (and let's be real, the mask can feel odd initially), but once you conquer your PADI Open Water Certification, you'll tap into an entire global community of dive sites that will have you feeling like Jacques Cousteau, but in way more stylish board shorts. Kick things off in a sun-kissed tropical paradise like Belize, Cozumel, or Thailand, or dive into lessons at your local dive shop. Scuba diving goes beyond just teaching you how to breathe deeply—it reveals the thrilling adventures lurking in corners of the world that most folks never glimpse. The vast ocean awaits. Time to gear up, my friend!

63

Try Rock Climbing Even If Heights Make You Sweat

There's something undeniably primal and exhilarating about gripping stone with just your fingers, toes, and a slightly questionable amount of faith in a harness. Rock climbing is the perfect cocktail of mental and physical challenge that requires more than just brute strength—it demands a delicate blend of balance, unwavering focus, and self-trust, one cautious reach at a time. If you're new to this wild adventure, kick things off at an indoor climbing gym—check out Mountain Project or The Climbing Business Journal to find one nearby—or consider signing up for a rookie outdoor course with REI Co-op Experiences or Outward Bound. You'll find an eclectic crew of fellow adventurers, all of whom share an unspoken camaraderie that comes from shouting "You got this!" while suspended 30 feet in the air. Each climb serves as a metaphor for life, and every summit stands as a testament that fear isn't something to avoid but rather something to power through. Remember, it's not about reaching the pinnacle every time—just focus on grabbing that next hold.

64

Ride in a Submarine Because the Ocean Has Secrets Just for You

Let's set the record straight: we're not chatting about a leisurely glass-bottom boat ride here. No, my friend, we're diving into the exhilarating world of a genuine submarine adventure. Think Bond, but with a twist of Cousteau—only this time, the snacks are top-notch, and your swagger is retirement-age cool. Companies like Atlantis Submarines whisk you away in places like Hawaii, Mexico, and the Caribbean, taking you on guided descents to over 100 feet beneath the waves. You'll glide through shipwrecks, coral gardens, and schools of wild fish, all while remaining warmly dry and comfortably cozy. Forget about shivering in a wetsuit; you're here to get up close and personal with a realm of our planet that most folks can only dream of exploring. If you're seeking an even bolder thrill, OceanGate Expeditions provides deep-sea research journeys aboard their state-of-the-art subs (when they're in operation). This isn't merely a sightseeing tour—it's a full-on plunge into the mysteries of the abyss. And as you resurface, squinting in the sunlight, you'll carry a unique treasure: the knowledge that you ventured into the depths—and returned transformed.

Stan Becomes a River God (Sort of) on the Ottawa River

At 65, Stan Whitaker considered himself a connoisseur of calm. He'd mastered the sacred arts of backyard grilling, rotating through a wardrobe of Hawaiian shirts, and kicking back in a beach chair with a cold beer and exactly zero responsibilities. Retirement, in theory, was his happy place.

But real life? That was a little more complicated.

Just six months out of his HR career, and newly divorced after 32 years of what he described as "lukewarm marital diplomacy"—Stan found himself floating through life like an inflatable pool toy. Directionless. Bored. Wondering if this was really it.

He rearranged the garage. Twice. He binge-watched an entire show about British baking and cried when the sourdough guy was eliminated. He tried pickleball. It was... fine. But everything felt like a slow crawl into the grave, just with better snacks.

Then came Jerry.

Jerry, his oldest buddy and chaos enthusiast, had zero interest in slow. He called one afternoon with the enthusiasm of a teenager who'd just discovered Red Bull and said, "You, me, and some angry Canadian rapids. Let's go whitewater rafting. Time to scream at some water."

Stan paused. "I'm too old to die wet and confused."

Jerry booked it anyway. OWL Rafting on the Ottawa River. Class III and IV rapids. Adventure-level chaos.

Two weeks later, Stan stood on the riverbank, squeezed into a neoprene wetsuit so tight it made him look like a retired seal with opinions about knee pain. He was surrounded by 20-somethings with names like Skylar and Blaze, all impossibly limber and unreasonably chipper at 7:00 a.m.

The guide gave a quick safety talk filled with words like "brace position" and "self-rescue." Stan was not comforted. His last brush with danger was trying to eat buffalo wings too soon after dental work.

Then the guide yelled, "Let's go!"

Stan climbed in, gripping his paddle like a man holding a steak knife in a bear fight.

Their first rapid was called Butcher's Knife, which felt overly honest.

The raft dipped into the torrent, and instantly, Stan's world exploded. He went right when the guide screamed left. Water blasted into his face. Blaze shrieked like a boy band fan at a farewell concert. Stan screamed too—like a man being mugged by Poseidon himself.

But then... something shifted.

The screaming turned into laughter. Not a nervous giggle, but a deep, primal, sweet-mother-of-adrenaline kind of laugh. The kind of laugh that wakes something up inside you that's been napping since Clinton was president.

By the second rapid, he was shouting "HARD PADDLE!" like he was storming Normandy. He high-fived strangers. He named his paddle. He got launched off the raft like a confused walrus, swallowed half the river, and still emerged grinning like a gladiator.

Skylar even fist-bumped him.

That night, back at camp, Stan sat by the fire, wrapped in a towel, sipping a cold beer that tasted like victory and river water. There was laughter all around, wet socks hanging from trees, and the kind of camaraderie that only comes from collectively surviving Mother Nature's washing machine.

But what Stan felt wasn't just adrenaline.

It was aliveness. The spark of confidence. The flicker of possibility. He wasn't washed up. He wasn't done. He'd out-paddled Blaze, dammit. He had mud in places that hadn't seen daylight in years, and he felt amazing.

He sent Jerry a text the next morning: "It's official. I'm a whitewater warlord. Let's ride again. Colorado next?"

And he meant it.

Final Thoughts: Your Comfort Zone Just Got a Lot Bigger

If you've made it this far, you've already done something legendary.

You dared to step out, speak up, and show up. You took risks not because you had to, but because something inside you whispered, *There's more.* And that whisper was right.

Bold adventures aren't always about crossing oceans or climbing mountains. Sometimes they're about crossing an invisible line—the one between who you've been and who you're still becoming. Each step out of the comfort zone cracked something open: courage, curiosity, maybe even a long-lost dream.

But now? Now it's time to channel that bold energy into something creative, meaningful, and lasting.

Because your next chapter isn't just about thrill—it's about craft. About discovering (or rediscovering) a passion that lights you up and gives your days a deeper spark. Whether it's learning photography, building an app, or finally writing that book, you're about to master something new. And in doing so, you'll master more of yourself.

Ready to turn boldness into brilliance?

Let's reignite your purpose.

CHAPTER 6

MASTER SOMETHING NEW—CREATIVE AND MODERN SKILLS TO REIGNITE PASSION AND PURPOSE

Welcome to the chapter where curiosity becomes your crown jewel. This is your invitation to explore new skills, stretch your creativity, and tap into passions you never had time for (or didn't even know you had). Whether you're learning to fly a drone, make sourdough that rivals Parisian bakers, build your own website, speak conversational Italian, or finally play Stairway to Heaven on the guitar—this is where purpose meets play.

And don't worry, nobody's expecting you to be a prodigy on day one. You're here to enjoy the process. To be a beginner again, but with better taste in wine and zero fear of failure.

So, sharpen your curiosity, roll up your sleeves, and let's reignite the fire.

The throne of lifelong learning is calling.

Learn to Play an Instrument Even if You Can't Read Music

Have you ever fantasized about strumming the guitar like the legendary Eric Clapton or crafting those silky smooth saxophone melodies reminiscent of John Coltrane? Well, stop dreaming and start doing! Now is the perfect moment to dive into the world of music. With innovative apps like Yousician and Fender Play, learning an instrument has transformed into an exhilarating experience that feels more like a video game than a chore. Local music shops are brimming with opportunities, offering everything from beginner classes to private lessons, tailored to suit your musical fancy. Whether you're itching to jam on a blues harmonica or tickle the ivories with some jazz piano, take heart in knowing that every single note you play is a step forward. Remember, it's never too late for you to discover your groove, unleash your inner rock star, and play the melodies that resonate with your soul. So, grab that instrument and let the music take you places you've only dreamed of before!

66

Start a Podcast (Yes, You Have Stories to Tell)

Do you have a treasure trove of opinions, with nuggets of wisdom mixed in, or perhaps some hilariously absurd stories that simply must escape the confines of your brilliant mind? Well, it's time to unleash that creative spirit! Snag a microphone, press that record button, and let the world hear your musings. Check out platforms like Buzzsprout or Anchor; they're the perfect launchpads for your podcasting adventure. Gather your friends for epic interviews, and dive into the things that get you buzzing—be it golf swings, culinary delights, globe-trotting tales, or the art of aging gracefully. Spice things up with a catchy title that rolls off the tongue, like Retired, Not Expired or The Dad Joke Hour. Remember, the magic formula here is equal parts creativity and a whole lot of connection. The result? A fulfilling journey that not only entertains but also enriches both your life and the lives of others. So, what are you waiting for? Grab that mic and let the adventures begin!

67

Enroll in a Welding or Blacksmithing Course

Engaging with fire and metal is an experience that offers a unique kind of gratification. Imagine taking a class at a local trade school or community center, where you can unleash your inner blacksmith. Institutions like The Crucible in Oakland or the John C. Campbell Folk School in North Carolina excel in offering immersive metalworking courses. Here, you'll have the opportunity to craft a knife that not only slices through tough meat but also turns heads at dinner parties. Or picture forging a bottle opener that not only cracks open your favorite brews but does so with a flair that screams craftsmanship. When you dive into the world of metalworking, you transform into that guy—the one who literally bends steel to his will. It's not merely a hobby for retirement; it's a channel for creativity that bestows upon you a sense of accomplishment and mastery. Embrace this fiery art, because wielding metal is not just a skill; it's a statement of power and self-reliance that few can claim.

68

Try Your Hand at Woodworking or Furniture Building

Picture this scenario: you meticulously carve a chair from a solid block of wood, sand it to perfection, and then plop down into it, casually proclaiming, "Yeah... I made that." There's something profoundly satisfying about woodworking; it's a slow, meditative craft that serves as a sanctuary for those who appreciate the art of creation. This isn't just a hobby; it's a grand adventure into the world of patience and focus—an ideal outlet for men who want to craft something meaningful and enduring. Whether you possess the skills of a seasoned carpenter or are just starting your journey, the world of woodworking awaits you. Seek out local workshops where you can learn from seasoned artisans or check out the Woodworkers Guild of America for resources and inspiration. And here's a little secret: When you whip up those handmade gifts for the grandkids, you'll instantly attain hero status in their eyes. Nothing beats the look of awe and admiration when they realize granddad made it just for them.

69

Dive Into Digital Photography and Editing

Pick up a DSLR or simply whip out your smartphone—either way, you're unlocking a treasure chest of creative possibilities. Dive into the realms of lighting, composition, and editing by taking courses on platforms like Skillshare or CreativeLive. Step outside, and stroll through your city with a fresh perspective—quite literally, as you experiment with new lenses. Share your stunning captures with others. Join invigorating photo challenges that push your creative boundaries. This isn't merely about snapping pictures; it's about experiencing life in ways you never imagined. Suddenly, that mundane street corner transforms into a canvas waiting for your artistic touch, and everyday moments become extraordinary stories that beg to be told. So, embrace this adventure, and let your imagination run wild as you discover the world anew through your camera lens. By doing so, you'll not only become a better photographer but also cultivate a deeper appreciation for the vibrant tapestry of life unfolding around you.

70

Grow a Garden Even on a Balcony

Gardening transcends mere digging; it's a delightful dance of design, experimentation, and therapeutic relief. Once you dive into the world of green thumbs, you'll find yourself knee-deep in creativity. From nurturing heirloom tomatoes bursting with flavor, shaping bonsai trees like a horticultural artist, to cultivating indoor succulents that bring a touch of nature inside, it's a slow craft that embodies the essence of life. It's your personal masterpiece, transforming from a patch of earth into a lush canvas. To streamline this earthy adventure, why not enlist the help of handy apps like Planter? These tools will keep your green endeavors organized, ensuring you know precisely what's thriving where. And the cherry on top? You'll soon find yourself armed with an abundance of fresh herbs, perhaps leading you to whip up a killer salsa recipe that'll have your friends asking for more. Gardening is more than just an outdoor hobby; it's a vibrant creation that takes root in your heart and soul.

71

LEARN THE ART OF LEATHERWORKING

Belts, wallets, knife sheaths, and journals—oh my! Leather crafting is the perfect blend of rugged charm and sophisticated elegance, and trust me, it has a way of becoming surprisingly addictive. You don't need to embark on this journey without a guide, either. Why not dive into the world of leather arts by snagging one of those beginner kits on Tandy Leather? If you're feeling particularly adventurous, consider signing up for a local makerspace class. Not only will you walk away with some impressive, usable, and gift-worthy creations, but you'll also get to enjoy a delightfully unique scent that wafts through your workshop; it's like the leather whispers, "Welcome to the club!" And let's not forget about the glorious therapeutic aspects of hand-stitching leather—it's like zen therapy for rebels. So grab a piece of leather, roll up your sleeves, and get ready to transform raw materials into something fantastic, all while honing your mad crafting skills.

72

Try Creative Writing (Fiction, Memoir, or Even a Children's Book)

Do you have a crazy tale from your younger days that's just itching to escape your brain? Maybe there's a quirky character who's taken up residence in your imagination, or perhaps you've learned some hard-hitting life lessons that are just begging to be shared with the world. Well, it's time to put pen to paper, my friend! Utilize brilliant tools like Scrivener or Dabble to wrangle those thoughts and give them some structure. Don't go it alone; hop into a writer's group at your local library or explore the vast landscape of the web with platforms like Scribophile. No matter if you're spinning a memoir or blasting off into the realms of science fiction, there's something truly magical about writing. It not only sharpens your mental faculties but also transforms scattered memories into coherent meaning. So, what are you waiting for? Get those words flowing and see where your creativity takes you!

73

Build a Tiny Home, Cabin, or Treehouse

If you happen to possess a stretch of land (or perhaps have a friend who's generously offering theirs), now's your golden opportunity to roll up your sleeves and construct something spectacular—entirely by yourself! YouTube is an endless treasure trove of instructional videos, helping you navigate everything from the basics to the advanced techniques of construction. Not to mention, companies like Backyard ADUs and Den Outdoors have jumped on the bandwagon with their prefab kits that make the entire process easier than ever. Imagine crafting your very own writing cabin, a cozy guest house for visitors, or even a swanky man cave nestled among the trees. It's not just about building something physical; it's the perfect combination of skill and freedom, allowing your creativity to soar. Plus, think of the bragging rights you'll have! Years down the line, while others merely talk about their dreams, you can proudly say, "I built that with my own two hands!" What could be more satisfying?

74

Take Up Drone Videography

This is the epitome of modern-day adventure—cinematic thrills wrapped in a wickedly fun package. First step? Get yourself a drone, perhaps a DJI Mini or something slick from B&H Photo. Once you have that little flying marvel in hand, it's time to dive into the fascinating world of aerial photography. Familiarize yourself with the rules of the skies, and you'll be ready to capture the world from angles you never thought possible. Picture this: soaring over majestic mountains, gliding along breathtaking coastlines, or even taking a bird's-eye view of your buddy's legendary BBQ where the grill is smoking and laughter fills the air. After you've worked your editing magic, throw those captivating clips up on YouTube or Instagram and watch as your followers marvel at your newfound aerial prowess. Trust me, retirement has never looked so jaw-dropping as it does from a lofty 400 feet in the air. This is your chance to redefine how you see and capture the world!

75

Make Your Own Hot Sauce, Wine, or Craft Beer

Creating your unique small-batch concoctions? Now that's what I call living the dream. Dive into the delightful world of home brewing with kits from Brooklyn Brew Shop or Uncommon Goods to kick off your adventure. Imagine the thrill of experimenting with fermentation, mastering the delicate art of flavor balance, and ultimately producing a one-of-a-kind beverage that's entirely yours. There's a certain charm in knowing that your creation can't be found anywhere else on this planet. And let's be honest, slapping a catchy label on it like "King's Inferno" or "Retired & Refined" instantly elevates your drink from mere hobby to something bordering on legendary status. Picture yourself impressing friends at a gathering, sipping a beverage you crafted, while you retell the tale of its creation. They'll undoubtedly be hanging onto every word, ready to try your exclusive brew. So, roll up your sleeves, unleash that inner alchemist, and enjoy the satisfaction that comes with crafting something truly extraordinary.

Learn Calligraphy or Digital Illustration

No matter if you're laying down ink with a classic pen or swiping a stylus across your tablet, engaging in calligraphy and illustration is not only a peaceful retreat but also a skill that turns heads. Picture this: you find yourself lost in the rhythmic swirls and loops of letters, or perhaps you're crafting intricate designs that could easily rival the masters. If you're looking to dive in, consider exploring apps like Procreate on an iPad, where your imagination can truly take flight. Alternatively, you can channel your inner artist through brush pen calligraphy via a plethora of online tutorials. The possibilities are endless! Picture yourself whipping up one-of-a-kind greeting cards, eye-catching logos, or those quirky personal mantras that can boldly proclaim your aspirations from above your workstation. Think of them as your creative battle flags, ready to rally your spirits! Not only does your artistic flair get sharper with each stroke, but your handwriting transforms into something that could make even the fonts on your computer weep with envy.

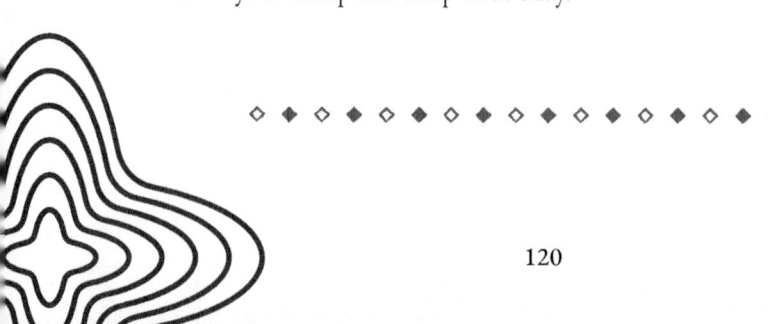

CREATE A YOUTUBE CHANNEL OR BLOG ABOUT YOUR PASSION

Whatever sparks your passion—be it globetrotting, tinkering with tools, whipping up gourmet dishes, or curating a collection of rare coins—you've got the ability to teach it. Share your knowledge, and in doing so, you'll build a vibrant community around your interests. Take advantage of platforms like Wix or Squarespace to kick-start your blog, or dive into YouTube Creator Studio to publish your videos. Not only will you expand your voice and hone your video editing skills, but you'll also connect with fellow enthusiasts from every corner of the globe who are just as excited about your passions as you are. This journey isn't just about learning; it's about achieving mastery in your craft while leaving a lasting legacy. So, whether you're documenting your travels, sharing a new recipe, or showcasing your coin collection, know that there's a whole world of people out there ready to join you on this adventure. Don't just enjoy your passions—celebrate them!

Leroy and the Legend of "Spicy Grandpa's Liquid Lightning"

When Leroy Henderson turned 70, his kids threw him a sweet backyard party: checkered tablecloths, a Costco sheet cake, and a plaque that read, "World's Best Grandpa."

Leroy smiled, posed for photos, and later that night, scraping frosting off his dentures, muttered, "You know what's better? World's Spiciest Grandpa."

While most slow down at 70, Leroy was just heating up. He wasn't your sweet-tea grandpa—he was the guy who carried hot sauce like others carried hand sanitizer. Glove box, tackle box, even once smuggling ghost pepper sauce into a Chili's because, as he said, "Their salsa's got less kick than a sleepy kitten."

When his buddy Ron mentioned a DIY hot sauce kit from *Uncommon Goods*, Leroy's eyes lit up. Within days, his kitchen became a spice lab—fermenting jars hissed, exotic chilies piled up like tiny grenades, and the fridge smelled strong enough to make the mailman cough.

Leroy studied YouTube gurus like "Capsaicin Cowboy," joined spicy forums as "ScovilleDaddy70," and imported peppers that came with legal waivers.

Batch one? Spoon-melter.

Batch two? Angry salsa.

Batch three? Floor spill that almost cost the dog his sniffer.

Batch four? Perfection.

Smoky, garlicky, a slow burn that sneaked up like a ninja. Leroy bottled it, slapped on a label of himself in a cape and shades, and named it:

"Spicy Grandpa's Liquid Lightning: Not Your Grandson's Ketchup."

At the family BBQ debut, his son-in-law cried, his granddaughter screamed, and neighbor Dale slathered it on everything, including ice cream.

Word spread.

His bridge club crowned him *The Heat King*. A food truck begged for a supply. His Etsy shop, *Capsaicin and Retirement*, sold out in a week. One buyer messaged: "This sauce made my husband cry and propose again. Bless you, Spicy Grandpa."

At 70, Leroy wasn't slowing down. He was just getting started.

Final Thoughts: Skill, Meet Soul

You did it. You gave yourself permission to be a beginner, to tinker, to try, and maybe even to fail fabulously. But more importantly, you rediscovered the magic of learning for yourself. No deadlines. No pressure. Just passion, play, and the kind of purpose that makes you jump out of bed with a grin.

Because mastering something new isn't about showing off. It's about showing up for your creativity, your joy, and the wide-open possibilities of your next chapter. Every chord you strummed, dish you plated, or app you coded chipped away at the myth that purpose ends with a paycheck.

But now? It's time to take that reignited spark and light up the world around you.

In the next chapter, we're turning inward growth into outward impact. Because real kings don't just rule—they uplift. From mentoring young minds to restoring community gardens, you'll explore powerful ways to serve, volunteer, and build a legacy that outlives you.

Let's go from personal passion to kingdom contribution.

CHAPTER 7

THE KING'S GIVEBACK—POWERFUL WAYS TO VOLUNTEER, SERVE, AND BUILD COMMUNITY

There's nothing more legendary than a man who uses his time, wisdom, and heart to make the world a little better than he found it. You've climbed the mountains, recharged your passion, mastered new skills, and now, it's time to pay it forward like the true King you are.

This chapter is your royal road map to purpose-driven impact. We're talking mentorship, community building, hands-on help, and unexpected ways to serve that go way beyond writing a check. Whether it's teaching teens how to build bikes, sharing stories at a local veterans' center, or growing veggies for a food bank, you're about to discover how powerful your presence can be.

You don't need a title to lead. You just need heart, time, and the willingness to say, "I'm here. How can I help?"

Because the King's legacy? It isn't measured in trophies. It's written in the lives he touches.

Let's build your legacy of kindness.

Mentor Young Entrepreneurs or Tradespeople

You've crafted a formidable career, navigated through the treacherous waters of economic downturns, made daring decisions, and, yes, learned from some less-than-stellar blunders. So, why not share that valuable treasure trove of wisdom you've gathered along the way? Organizations such as SCORE, Junior Achievement, or local trade schools are perpetually on the lookout for experienced mentors to guide the next generation. Picture this: you step into a room filled with eager young minds, their eyes sparkling with curiosity, ready and willing to absorb all the hard-earned knowledge you've fought so hard to acquire. And here's the kicker—while you're imparting your life lessons, these bright youngsters will also be more than happy to enlighten you about the latest TikTok trends and viral dances. You might even find yourself ready to join the next viral challenge. So, grab this opportunity to bridge the gap between generations, swap wisdom for fresh perspective, and enjoy a few laughs along the way. Your expertise could be just the spark they need!

79

VOLUNTEER AT A LOCAL FOOD BANK AND STAY FOR THE STORIES

Food banks are in dire need of hands, but let's not overlook the power of mere presence. Donning an apron and spending a few hours sorting through goods or distributing hot meals won't just leave your feet aching; it'll grant you a brand-new perspective on life. When you lend a helping hand, take a moment to connect with the people you're serving—they each have a story to tell, rich with experiences that paint a vivid picture of resilience and determination. One minute, you might hear about a shared struggle, and the next, you'll be chuckling over a lighthearted joke that reminds you of our shared humanity. If you're uncertain where to begin, a quick trip to Feeding America's site will pinpoint a food bank in your area faster than you can say "how can I help?" Roll up your sleeves and dive in—there's no better way to understand the world around you than to step right into it, one meal, one story, one laugh at a time.

80

Join a Habitat for Humanity Build (Swing That Hammer With Purpose)

This is community service that builds character and calluses. You'll not only construct homes but also forge friendships and ignite real change in your community. As you swing hammers and assemble walls, you'll pick up construction hacks you never knew were missing from your life. Are you worried about your lack of experience? Don't sweat it! Habitat volunteers team up with skilled professionals who will guide you every step of the way. It's a chance to roll up your sleeves and learn while making a tangible difference. Whether you're in the heart of a bustling city or a quaint little town, check out Habitat for Humanity for opportunities around the globe. And here's a little secret: after a long day of hard work, that reward beer you crack open hits differently—it's nothing short of legendary. So, come on, let's turn those blisters into badges of honor as you dive into a fulfilling experience that promises laughter, camaraderie, and a sense of accomplishment!

81

Coach a Youth Sports Team or After-School Club

You don't have to be the next Vince Lombardi, just someone who can show up, offer a word of encouragement, and knows how to throw a decent spiral—or at least act like you do. Community organizations like youth leagues, chess clubs, robotics teams, and coding camps are perpetually on the lookout for volunteer coaches or mentors who can inspire young minds. Think about trying the YMCA, Boys & Girls Clubs, or your local recreation center. You might be taken aback by how incredible it feels to share a high-five with a kid who just nailed a layup—all because you believed in them when they thought they couldn't. It's not just about winning or losing; it's about fostering confidence and perseverance. You'll find that your enthusiasm can ignite a spark in these kids, making a real difference in their lives. So, dust off those old cleats or that forgotten chess set, and get in the game—both you and the kids are bound to learn something valuable in the process.

82

BE A HOSPITAL OR HOSPICE VOLUNTEER (PRESENCE IS POWER)

Occasionally, the true essence of giving back is far from the spotlight—it's more akin to a whisper than a shout, a hallowed engagement that taps into our shared humanity. Hospitals and hospices are often in search of volunteers who can lend a compassionate ear to patients, offer comforting conversations to families, or simply share the silence with those who might be lonely. If you're keen on making a profound impact, consider checking out the Hospice Foundation of America or your local health network. That's the kind of soul work that doesn't just fill a schedule, but genuinely enriches lives. While some might feel inclined to think that making a difference requires grand gestures, remember that sometimes, the most meaningful contributions manifest in humble ways. Investing your time in this manner could very well be one of the most significant and fulfilling things you ever undertake. So, if you have a moment or two to spare, why not turn your attention to the heart of humanity? It's an experience worth having.

83

VOLUNTEER WITH VETERANS' ORGANIZATIONS

Show your appreciation for our heroes by dedicating some of your valuable time to organizations like the Wounded Warrior Project, Team Rubicon, or The American Legion. These groups are always on the lookout for helping hands, whether it's providing transportation, lending a friendly ear, or sharing expert advice on transitioning to civilian work. The need is real, and your contributions can truly make a difference. By engaging with these remarkable individuals, you'll encounter extraordinary men and women whose life experiences could make even the most riveting tales in your repertoire seem mundane. There's a bond that forms amid shared service, and in giving back, you'll not only uplift others but also enrich your own life. You'll discover that the camaraderie developed through these initiatives can lead to friendships that last a lifetime, all while providing support to those who have sacrificed so much for our freedom. In every moment you give, you'll find mutual respect and stories that echo long after you've parted ways.

84

TEACH FINANCIAL LITERACY OR LIFE SKILLS TO TEENS

You've mastered the art of budgeting, skillfully dodging scams, navigating the treacherous waters of tax filing, and buying a car without being taken for a ride. To most teenagers, you might as well have a magic wand in your hand. Why not pass on that impressive wisdom? Think about volunteering at a local school, an after-school program, or even joining forces with organizations like Operation HOPE. You have the chance to teach these young minds the crucial life skills that aren't covered in their textbooks. Imagine the impact you could have just by breaking down the mysteries of compound interest or shedding light on how credit scores influence their financial futures. You might be surprised to discover that your insights can alter the trajectory of someone's life. They might walk out of your session armed with knowledge and confidence that will serve them well into adulthood. You have the ability to shape their understanding of money and perhaps ignite a passion for financial literacy that lasts a lifetime.

85

SERVE AT A COMMUNITY GARDEN OR URBAN FARM

Getting down and dirty with a purpose? Now that's what I call therapy—plus a side of community service. Community gardens do more than just fill bellies; they're the unsung heroes that tackle food insecurity, transform bland neighborhoods into vibrant spaces, and create connections among folks from all walks of life. If you're itching to get involved, hop on over to AmpleHarvest.org or connect with a local garden collective near you. You'll end up mingling with a fabulous mix of people—kids, grandparents, and everyone in between—while snagging some fresh, mouth-watering veggies that you can brag about at dinner parties. Who knows? You might even plant something that'll nourish not just your family but generations to come. And let's be honest, nothing says "I'm living my best life" quite like having dirt under your nails. So, grab that spade and let's dig into this earthy adventure; it's good for the soul and the community!

86

HELP BUILD ACCESSIBILITY FOR SENIORS OR PEOPLE WITH DISABILITIES

Organizations such as Rebuilding Together provide fantastic opportunities to enhance homes with features like ramps, safety rails, and wider doorways. Imagine the impact of a few hours of your time, armed with nothing but a wrench and a dash of determination. You can completely revolutionize someone's independence, making it a noble pursuit indeed! It's a bit like being a superhero, but instead of a cape, you'll don a tool belt and wield a power drill. So, roll up those sleeves, channel your inner handyman, and feel the satisfaction of transforming someone's life right before your eyes. After all, you've got what it takes: hands ready for action, tools at the ready, and a bit of spare time on your hands. Why not put them to use in a way that leaves a lasting imprint—literally? Every little adjustment you make not only alters a living space but also uplifts the spirit of those who call it home. Now, that's a legacy worth building!

Start or Join a Local Litter Cleanup or Beautification Crew

Put on those gloves, grab a trash bag, and rally a few of your friendly neighbors. It's time for an adventure! Stroll through the trails, give the beach a good spruce up, and breathe new life into the park. You don't need some grand organization to kick off your mission; all you need is a willingness to make a difference. However, if you prefer to team up with the pros, look no further than initiatives like Keep America Beautiful or Adopt-a-Highway. Joining forces can amplify your impact, and let's be honest, it feels pretty great to do something meaningful. Plus, it's an excellent excuse to get those steps in, soak up some fresh air, and enjoy a view that you know looks just a little better because of your efforts. So, lace up those shoes and make the world a cleaner, greener place one step at a time. Who knew doing good could feel this good?

88

BECOME A READING BUDDY OR LITERACY VOLUNTEER

Reading has a remarkable power to transform lives, yet not every child—or adult, for that matter—receives the guidance they truly need. It's time to step up and lend a hand! Join forces with organizations like Reading Partners, Literacy Volunteers of America, or even your neighborhood library. When you volunteer, you're doing far more than just imparting knowledge about words; you're igniting a spark of self-assurance in those you help. Imagine this: dedicating just 10 minutes a day could be the tipping point for someone finally understanding that they've got what it takes to complete their education. That moment of clarity, that realization—now *that's* a legacy worth leaving behind! You're not just changing a life; you're becoming the reason someone else believes in their own intelligence and capabilities. So, why not trade some spare time for a cause that pays dividends in newfound confidence and opportunity? After all, your contributions could be the miracle they were waiting for!

89

VOLUNTEER AT AN ANIMAL SHELTER OR WILDLIFE RESCUE

Dogs, cats, owls, raccoons—your imagination can run wild with the choices! When you volunteer at animal shelters, you're not just picking up a mop or a leash; you're stepping into a realm where every day is filled with furry cuddles and the kind of affection that makes your heart do a little jig. Picture this: you walk the dogs who are eager to strut their stuff, channeling their inner runway model while you're on cleanup duty, getting the kennels in tip-top shape. Toss in some kibble for the adorable little orphans, and voilà—you're officially a superhero in the eyes of those furry companions. Consider lending a hand at places like Best Friends Animal Society, or checking out your local humane society. Not only do you get to dish out treats and belly rubs, but you also experience the joy of those enthusiastic tail wags and soothing purrs. And who knows? You might just end up finding your new best friend waiting for you behind the bars, ready to embark on countless adventures together.

Gary Builds More Than Just Walls With Habitat for Humanity

Gary Mendoza was 66, retired from teaching high school shop class, and feeling just a little too familiar with his La-Z-Boy recliner. One afternoon, after watching an entire documentary on how paint dries (it was actually about paint chemistry, but still), he realized something: He missed building stuff. Not just birdhouses or fixing the leaky garage roof—real, meaningful, hands-dirty kind of building.

Then his daughter sent him a link to Habitat for Humanity with a little note that said: "Still got it, Dad?"

Challenge accepted.

The next weekend, Gary showed up at a build site on the edge of town, not knowing what to expect. He was half-convinced it would be a bunch of young people in yoga pants holding clipboards. Instead, he found a ragtag crew of retirees, local college students, and one guy named Phil who had no idea how to use a nail gun but made a killer sandwich spread.

Gary got paired with a team framing a new home for a single mom and her two kids. He hadn't worked this hard in years, and he loved it. His hands were sore, his back ached, and there was sawdust in places sawdust shouldn't be—but man, did he feel alive. He taught a few people how to use a circular saw properly, learned how to install hurricane clips (who knew?), and even traded dad jokes with a 22-year-old who called him "G-Money."

At the end of the week, they raised the final wall, and the family showed up with tears in their eyes. Gary stood there, hammer in hand, chest puffed with pride—not because he built a house, but because he helped build a home.

That night, as he cracked open a cold beer with the crew, sunburned and smiling, Gary said, "That was the best damn day I've had in ten years." And he meant it.

Final Thoughts: Your Crown Shines Brightest When Shared

You didn't just give back—you gave forward. You showed up, offered your time, your talents, your stories, and made the world feel a little more connected, a little more human, and a whole lot more hopeful.

That's what real kings do. They don't rule from thrones—they rise by lifting others. Whether you planted kindness in a garden, mentored someone through a storm, or helped rebuild a community space brick by brick, you've proven that giving isn't just noble—it's transformational.

But before you polish your crown and call it a day, there's one more chapter waiting, and this one's got dust on its boots and adventure in its eyes.

Because next? We go rogue in the best way possible.

It's time to tap into your wild side. The spontaneous road trips. The midnight flights. The no-plan weekends that lead to the best stories. It's about chasing joy without a GPS and trusting the road to show you something unexpected.

So pack light, bring your freedom-loving heart, and let's finish strong.

Your next great adventure is waiting, King.

CHAPTER 8

WANDER BOLDLY—WILD AND SPONTANEOUS ADVENTURES FOR THE OPEN-ROAD SOUL

Let's be honest: Some of life's greatest moments come when you veer completely off script.

This chapter is for the retired King who knows that freedom isn't just about having time—it's about having the guts to use it wildly. No strict itineraries, no laminated checklists—just open roads, open hearts, and the thrill of not knowing exactly what's around the corner.

Whether it's hopping in your camper van with nothing but snacks and a playlist, chasing small-town festivals you didn't plan to attend, or booking a last-minute train to somewhere you've never heard of—this is where your spontaneous soul gets to dance.

We'll explore quirky road trips, rail-pass adventures, mystery vacations (yes, those exist!), and the pure joy of saying "Why not?" instead of "Maybe someday." This isn't about being reckless. It's about being recklessly present.

Because you've earned your freedom. Now, it's time to enjoy the ride.

90: Take a Route-Free Van or RV Road Trip

No reservations necessary. Forget the spreadsheets; it's just you, some gas, snacks, and a vague notion of where the sunsets paint the sky. Rent a campervan loaded with all the essentials from Outdoorsy or Escape Campervans, or go all out and personalize your own RV before you hit the highway. Imagine waking up beside a serene river, pitching your tent under majestic red rock formations, or taking a refreshing shower with the stunning Pacific Ocean as your backdrop. When you're on the road without a fixed destination, every turn can lead to an unexpected adventure. And that first cup of coffee brewed right there on your tailgate? That's the essence of ultimate freedom. Embrace the open road, let the breeze guide you, and watch as the world unfolds in front of you, filled with spontaneous stops and serendipitous encounters. Forget the itinerary! It's time to explore, unwind, and make memories that are truly unforgettable.

91

Cross a Continent by Train and Let the World Unfold Outside Your Window

Nothing quite compares to the sheer joy of witnessing landscapes transform before your eyes while your only task is to leisurely sip tea in the dining car. Picture yourself on iconic journeys like the Rocky Mountaineer in Canada, the Trans-Siberian Railway carving its way across Russia, or The Ghan winding through the heart of Australia. There's something uniquely special about trains; they encourage you to slow down and savor the experience in the absolute best way possible. You'll cross paths with locals whose lives are as rich as the scenery, embark on mini-adventures through bustling stations reminiscent of Indiana Jones, and roll into new cities feeling refreshed and brimming with captivating stories to share. Each mile is a narrative unfolding, and every stop is a chance to explore a new chapter in your journey. So, let the rhythmic clatter of the tracks lull you into a state of blissful relaxation, and prepare for an escapade filled with unforgettable moments.

92

SAY YES TO A HOT AIR BALLOON SAFARI

Soar to new heights as the sun peeks over the horizon in stunning landscapes like Tanzania's Serengeti, Turkey's enchanting Cappadocia, or the sprawling vistas of New Mexico's Rio Grande Valley. Picture this: balloon safaris that are equal parts graceful glide and mind-bending spectacle. It's not just flying; it's an experience that defies logic and gravity. Enlist the pros through esteemed companies like Serengeti Balloon Safaris or Butterfly Balloons in Cappadocia, where the magic truly comes alive. Imagine gently floating in utter silence, high above a herd of majestic elephants or the whimsical fairy chimneys that dot the Cappadocian landscape. You'll feel the adrenaline rush and the goosebumps creeping up your spine, a bucket-list moment that's begging to be savored. Each flight is a blend of tranquility and exhilaration, offering a unique perspective that's sure to leave you breathless. So, grab your camera and prepare for an adventure that promises unforgettable memories and stunning vistas from the sky.

93

GO ISLAND HOPPING WITH JUST A BACKPACK AND A MAP

Imagine yourself meandering through the sun-drenched islands of Greece, the pristine beaches of the Philippines, or the laid-back charm of the South Pacific. There's a certain magic in the art of slow travel, and few things embody that better than hopping from one island to the next on a ferry. Say goodbye to the hustle of traditional itineraries; instead, cozy up in a quaint guesthouse, savoring the tantalizing taste of freshly caught seafood right by the shore. Ditch the glossy travel blogs, and pay attention to those in the know—the locals! They hold the keys to hidden gems and authentic experiences that you won't find in any guidebook. For a rough idea of your route, check out useful sites like Rome2Rio or Ferryhopper, but don't get too attached to those plans. Toss that map aside and let the salty breeze guide your adventures. Picture this: a carefree vibe, the refreshing kiss of sea spray on your skin, and the promise of a sun-kissed tan that turns heads wherever you go.

◇ ♦ ◇ ♦ ◇ ♦ ◇ ♦ ◇ ♦ ◇ ♦ ◇ ♦ ◇ ♦ ◇

94

Book a One-Way Ticket and Figure It Out Later

This is spontaneity at its peak, my friends. Picture this: you've got your sights set on a city that's always been on your bucket list—Lisbon, where the cobblestones echo stories of the past? Or perhaps the neon-laced streets of Tokyo, buzzing with life? Maybe you're dreaming of savoring street tacos in Mexico City? Grab a one-way ticket—no turning back now! Ditch the mainstream hotels and nestle into a cozy Airbnb run by locals; they know all the hidden gems. Forget Google Maps; let your feet be your compass as you meander through charming side streets. Chuck the rigid itinerary and embrace the delightful unpredictability of wandering. Strike up conversations with the locals; they'll gladly share their favorite eateries—who cares if you don't speak the language? Here's the kicker: Liberation comes not from knowing what's around the corner but from the thrill of embracing the unknown. This is the adventure that most folks shy away from, but for you? It's just the beginning.

95

SLEEP IN UNUSUAL PLACES AROUND THE WORLD

Trade conventional hotels for unforgettable experiences. Imagine curling up in a treehouse high above Bali's lush canopy, or nestling into a cozy yurt under the vast Mongolian sky. Picture yourself thawing out in an ice hotel in Sweden, sipping warm cocoa as frost adorns your surroundings, or exploring the surreal cave hotels of Cappadocia, where ancient rock formations create an enchanting backdrop. Platforms like Canopy & Stars, Airbnb, and Glamping Hub offer a range of options that fit your wildest dreams. Each unique stay is its own adventure, seamlessly mixing comfort with a delightful dash of whimsy. These accommodations aren't just places to rest your head—they're invitation cards to the most incredible stories waiting to unfold. You'll gather tales that friends will envy, just by choosing the right spot to lie down at night. So, pack your bags and prepare for some serious fun; your next great story is only a night away.

96

Hop on a Cargo Ship Adventure

Absolutely, you can hop aboard a functioning cargo ship and experience life at sea in all its gritty glory. Forget the luxury of poolside cabanas and the cringe of nightly karaoke; this is the real deal. With companies like Cargo Ship Voyages and Freighter Expeditions, you can embark on journeys that stretch from just a few days to several weeks. Picture it: sharing meals with the crew, soaking up their stories, and immersing yourself in the daily rhythm of life on the water. It's like stepping into a living postcard, where every wave feels like an adventure waiting to unfold. Time becomes a fluid concept as you trade the hustle and bustle of daily life for a more serene, unscripted existence. Plus, you can wave goodbye to the throngs of tourists who usually crowd the hotspots—there's something liberating about being out there, far from the selfie sticks and gift shops. Your cargo ship adventure promises unforgettable experiences and stories that will make your friends green with envy.

97

Follow a Festival Trail (And Let Music Guide You)

Set off on an adventure through the vibrant rhythms and vivid colors of nations far and wide. Picture yourself at Portugal's booming Boom Festival, where the air buzzes with the sounds of creativity and connection. Then, journey to Morocco for the enchanting Gnaoua World Music Festival, where every note weaves its magic into the fabric of a shared experience. Each festival serves as a breadcrumb along your path, leading you through cultures that are as rich and diverse as the spices in a Moroccan souk. So, pitch your tent under a starlit sky, revel in the freedom of dancing with bare feet on the earth, and gather around with newfound companions. Let the sound of distant drums summon the spirit of community, as laughter mingles with the melodies of joyful gatherings. Allow the rhythm of the music to guide you like a compass, and let joy be your unwavering map as you explore the world, one festival at a time.

98

Travel by Horseback in a Remote Destination

Embark on a grand adventure, galloping through untamed landscapes as nobility did in days of yore. Picture yourself on a horse trek in the breathtaking realms of Patagonia, the endless steppes of Mongolia, or the rugged terrain of the Wild West, all curated by renowned outfitters such as The Long Riders Guild or Estancia Huechahue in Argentina. Here, the world unfolds at a leisurely pace, allowing you to absorb the stunning scenery and immerse yourself in the natural world in a manner that's entirely organic—no engine can match this authentic experience. Feel the wind whip through your hair as you traverse mountains, valleys, and plains, creating bonds with both your steed and the earth beneath you. It's a journey that offers not just a ride but a profound connection to history, nature, and the wild spirit of exploration. So, saddle up and let your soul roam free; adventure awaits in every hoofbeat.

99

Do a Walking Pilgrimage (Sacred or Secular)

Walk with intention, and you'll find that every step shifts something within you. Consider taking on the legendary Camino de Santiago in Spain, where centuries of footsteps have carved a path rich with history and camaraderie. Alternatively, the enchanting Kumano Kodo in Japan offers a breathtaking blend of spiritual heritage and natural beauty that's hard to resist. If international travel isn't in your cards, fret not! There are coast-to-coast trails right in your backyard that promise their own unique adventures. When you embark on these journeys, carry only the essentials; this isn't a game of pack mule but a quest for enlightenment. Sleep at cozy, shared inns where the stories of fellow travelers become part of the adventure. As your feet hit the trail, something magical happens—the rhythm of your footsteps begins to quiet the chaos within. You'll encounter fellow wanderers, each with their own tales to share, and by the time you cross the final mile, something profound settles in your soul that's worth every step taken.

100

Embark on a Culinary Road Trip— One Bite at a Time

Select a theme—whether it's tacos, BBQ, doughnuts, regional wines, or diners boasting questionable signage but stellar reviews—and craft your adventure around it. Picture this: a road trip that spans across a state or country, making pit stops at every hidden gem, food truck, roadside shack, or beloved mom-and-pop café that embodies your culinary quest. Utilize apps like Roadfood, TVFoodMaps, or dive into local Reddit threads to discover gastronomic treasures that people rave about. Don't just settle for tasting; engage with the cooks themselves. Inquire about their secret sauces or special recipes. Make this a jubilant and delicious pilgrimage to food heaven. Remember, food is more than just nourishment; it's a slice of culture, a way to connect with people, and on the right journey, it morphs into your favorite tale. Pro tip: Bring along a journal to rate each stop as if you're the fiercest food critic on the planet—no filters, just pure unadulterated passion!

101

Book a "Mystery Trip" and Let the Surprise Take You

Surrender all notions of control and plunge headfirst into a curated surprise adventure. Enter the realm of companies like Pack Up + Go, Magical Mystery Tours, and Journee, where they take the reins and craft entire trips without spilling the beans on your destination until you've landed at the airport. Imagine the thrill as you receive cryptic clues, packing tips, and a surge of excitement reminiscent of childhood days spent unwrapping birthday presents. Why embark on this whimsical journey? Because there's a certain magic in spontaneity that jolts your senses awake, rekindling that childlike wonder tucked away since those carefree days. It's a delightful reminder that some of life's most remarkable escapades are the ones that remain unplanned. Let go of the spreadsheets and itineraries; instead, embrace the adventure of the unknown. Dive into the excitement, and let the mystery unfold as you discover new horizons, experiences, and perhaps even aspects of yourself you never knew existed.

102

Sunset-to-Sunrise Marathon

Pack a thermos filled to the brim with your favorite coffee, hit the open road as the sun dips below the horizon, and make a solemn vow to chase that mesmerizing line of dusk all through the night. Embrace spontaneity as you stop at random destinations along the way: Find yourself at a midnight diner where the coffee flows as freely as the conversation, or wander to an empty beach where the sound of waves serenades the stars. Dive into a small-town bar illuminated by flickering neon beer signs and strike up conversations with the locals, who are likely more interesting than they appear. If the spirit moves you, take a quick nap under the expansive night sky, letting the cosmos be your blanket. As dawn breaks, awaken in a place you've never laid eyes on before, and if you're really feeling adventurous, don't forget to brush your teeth in the charmingly rustic confines of a gas station bathroom. Bonus points if it has an ambiance that inspires life decisions! Use AllStays to discover those 24-hour hotspots and safe overnight stops that can make your road trip an unforgettable adventure.

103

Mystery Food Crawl

Choose a nearby town that's been flying under your radar; the kind of place you've zipped past but haven't given a second thought. Hop in your car and set off with one golden rule: You can only indulge in culinary experiences at establishments you've never heard of before. Upon arrival, tap into the local wisdom by engaging with random residents. Pose questions like, "Where do you go when you want to escape the tourist herd?" or "If your coolest cousin came to town, where would you send him for the ultimate meal?" This is your chance to explore the hidden gems of the culinary world. Sample intriguing snacks, artisanal beverages, hearty meals, or indulgent desserts, and don't shy away from the dishes with names that are impossible to pronounce. The thrill of discovering something truly unfamiliar is part of the adventure. You might even check out websites like Atlas Obscura for tips on secret foodie spots that are off the beaten path. Embrace the unknown, and let your taste buds do the exploring!

Walt Finds His Altitude and His Inner Poet in Cappadocia

Walt Preston, 69, was the kind of guy who used to think "sky-high adventure" meant getting a senior discount on aisle seats. A retired postmaster from Cincinnati, Walt had spent his life on solid ground, sorting letters, mowing his lawn in perfect lines, and never missing a 6:00 p.m. dinner. But after his grandkids gifted him a "Bucket List Scratch-Off Map," something in him shifted. One square read: Hot Air Balloon Ride Over Cappadocia, Turkey.

"Sounds like something for Instagram influencers," Walt muttered—then promptly booked it.

One month later, there he was, in the pre-dawn hush of Göreme National Park, sipping strong Turkish coffee while staring at dozens of balloons being inflated like giant, sleepy dragons waking up. The air was crisp. The anticipation? Electric.

The moment his balloon lifted off, everything went silent.

Below him, the surreal rock spires—called fairy chimneys—glowed orange under the rising sun. Walt hovered above valleys and ancient cave dwellings, gliding like a bird in slow motion. It wasn't just scenic. It was spiritual. He wasn't thinking about cholesterol or lawn fertilizer. He was breathing in beauty. Feeling small, yet limitless.

A fellow passenger asked him how it felt.

Walt looked down at the floating shadows and said, "Like I left my worries on the ground... and they didn't follow me up."

When they landed (smooth as silk), they toasted with champagne—a ballooning tradition. Walt, who once claimed writing wasn't his thing, scribbled that quote into a notebook that night. He's been journaling ever since.

He now refers to that trip as "The Day Gravity Took a Break." And every time someone complains about aging, he pulls out his phone and shows a photo of himself, wind in his hair, above the clouds.

Final Thoughts: The Road Doesn't End—It Expands

You wandered. Boldly. Bravely. Maybe even barefoot on a beach you didn't plan to visit.

You said yes to detours, followed hunches, trusted your gut, and proved—once again—that the best stories aren't always the ones you planned. They're the ones where you rolled down the window, turned up the music, and let life surprise you.

And that's the thing: Retirement doesn't mean the road ends. It means you finally get to choose where it goes.

So, here you are, King—no crown required, no map necessary. Just you, your passions, your people, and the wide open everything ahead. You've redefined what retirement can be: thrilling, meaningful, a little wild, and wildly yours.

You've laughed. You've grown. You've given back. And now? You're just getting started.

Because legends don't retire. They reign with heart.

Keep wandering, keep daring, and most of all—keep living like the King you are!

The Royal Planner: The Year of Legendary Adventures

Congratulations, Your Majesty—you've officially claimed your throne in the Land of Legendary Living. But even a king needs a little nudge now and then to keep the kingdom exciting.

Enter *The Royal Planner*: your official scroll of 12 mini-missions—one daring, delightful quest for each month of the year. Think of it as your personal blueprint for banishing boredom and crafting a life story worth bragging about at every castle feast (or, you know, Sunday brunch).

In this downloadable bonus, you'll find

- ◊ checklists to keep the excitement alive because ticking a box feels way more satisfying than you think.

- ◊ a notes section to plot your next escapades, record your victories, or reflect on the occasional misadventure (those are the best stories, after all).

- ◊ a Reward system filled with tongue-in-cheek prizes after trying something mildly terrifying (hello, zip lining!).

Each mini-mission is inspired by the big, bold ideas in this book, but with even more permission to get creative, go rogue, and laugh along the way. Let's get your Royal Year started.

ENJOY RETIREMENT LIKE A KING

SCAN TO CLAIM YOUR
ROYAL PLANNER

ROYAL BONUS

CONCLUSION

LONG LIVE THE KING OF RETIREMENT

Well, Your Majesty, you made it.

You've now got access to 103 unforgettable ways to not just retire, but to reign. Boldly. Creatively. Unapologetically.

This book was never about slowing down. It was about stepping into your prime. You now have permission to ditch the ordinary and design a life that's rich with adventure, purpose, and a damn good story or two. And the best part? You can return to these pages anytime. These ideas aren't going anywhere, but you are.

You're embracing freedom and adventure, carving new paths with the kind of spontaneity that makes life exciting again. From last-minute road trips to sky-high thrills, the world is open—and it's waiting for you.

You're creating joy through connection, building real friendships, throwing epic game nights, and laughing until your stomach hurts. Because life, after all, is best enjoyed together.

You're pursuing lifelong learning, proving that passion has no age limit. From mastering the guitar to trying your hand at drone photography, every new skill adds another jewel to your crown.

And you're choosing to share your journey, inspiring others to live bigger, love deeper, and say yes more often.

So here's the final royal decree:

- ◊ Keep exploring.
- ◊ Keep laughing.
- ◊ Keep saying, "Why not?"

Because the only limit now is the horizon.

If you enjoyed this book, please leave a review. And why not detail which adventure lit you up the most or sparked your next big move? Your words might just inspire the next King in waiting.

And hey—if you happen to know an amazing woman in your life who's approaching retirement (or already rocking it), don't let her miss out on the fun. Send her over to check out our companion guide: *103 Fun Ways to Enjoy Retirement Like a Queen.*

Retirement isn't the end. It's the ultimate beginning. Here's to living like royalty—on your own terms.

REFERENCES

This book was inspired by curiosity, reinvention, and a refusal to grow bored. Some ideas were drawn from publicly available sources, including:

- ◊ RTOERO – Wondering what to do in retirement?
- ◊ Boldin – 120 Big Ideas for Retirement
- ◊ Unbiased – 25 Things to Do in Retirement
- ◊ Worldpackers – Bucket List Adventures
- ◊ Particle for Men – Hobbies & Activities After 50
- ◊ Second Wind Movement – How to Be Adventurous After 60
- ◊ Verywell Mind – Tips for Adjusting to Retirement
- ◊ Condé Nast Traveler – Most Adventurous Experiences

- ◊ Annuity.org – Retirement Bucket List Ideas
- ◊ Hero Health – The Ultimate Retirement Bucket List
- ◊ LinkedIn – Mental Health After Retirement

All trademarks, program names, and organization names are the property of their respective owners and are used here for illustrative and educational purposes only.